November 5, 2013

Steve & Donna,

Life is short, take time to enjoy the journey. I value our friendship & thank both of you for helping me "up the ladder". If we move in the direction of our dreams, our dreams will become a successful reality.

With my love & respect,

Up the Ladder to Success

Good Times, Hard Times,
But Never Bad Times

By McKenzie "Ken" Cook

Copyright © 2012 McKenzie Cook

Published by LifeWriter Personal Histories
PO Box 1290
Albany, OR 97321
life-writer.com

ISBN 978-1-4675-5202-8
Independent Publisher

Printed in the United States of America

Dedication

This undertaking would not have been possible without my mother and father, to whom I am thankful for bringing me into this world. They gave me the strength, direction, motivation and commitment to pick myself up in defeat and maintain a positive mental attitude. Thank you, Mom and Dad.

I was blessed with two wonderful brothers, Richard and Donn, and a sister, Marilyn, who made my early days on Marquam Hill a dream come true. Life was simple, and we gave of ourselves to make it better. As a family we stayed together, shared and learned from each other, and to this day we love and respect each other. We all cherish the memories.

As always, enduring gratitude to my many friends from Portland, Oregon, Escondido, California, Corvallis, Oregon, San Diego, California, Minneapolis, Minnesota, and Welches, Oregon. True friendships are forever. My mentors and special friends in my "Up-the-Ladder" Hall of Fame have made me who I am today. Thank you for trusting me, thank you for being there for me, and thank you for your friendship. My passion has been to help others and multiply all that God has given me, and in the process, to give back more than I have received.

Lastly, I acknowledge my beautiful wife, Mary Lou, who mothered our four children, Amy, Tom, Allison and Caroline. She has been a wonderful, caring mother, a loving and giving wife, a woman of patience and good judgment, and the focus of my love and devotion for 52 years.

My story is unique and personal, but it reflects the classic American dream: family, love, hardship, vision, determination, entrepreneurial struggle, success, and happiness. Mary Lou and I have spent hundreds of hours writing this story, and it has been a most enjoyable experience. With thanks and respect, I dedicate this book to my loving wife, Mary Lou, and to our four children, Amy, Tom, Allison and Caroline.

McKenzie "Ken" Cook

Contents

Family Background

The quotes that appear in this book are from the personal collection of McKenzie Cook.

McKenzie Cook's Up-the-Ladder Team

CAREY & JOHN ANDERSON AND TOM COOK

JERRY HALAMUDA

GARY BISHOP

NORM OSBORNE

PAT KEIG

MYRON EICHEN

JIM HINES

TOM EWING

RED SCOTT

DAVE COX

MONTE FRODSHAM

GUS KUEHLER

ANTONIO SACCONAGHI

MARY LOU MCROBERTS COOK

MR. AND MRS. HAROLD D. COOK

With my respect and sincere appreciation.

I BELIEVE *that life's encounters are the rungs on a ladder to success. As we're ascending, we meet people who play a variety of important roles in influencing our progress. My life has been blessed with friends and mentors who have enriched my journey in countless ways.*

No one's ladder leads directly upward without some brief pauses and a few steps backward. I wouldn't be where I am today without the crises and failures that are thoroughly interspersed with my successes. With every setback, we get the chance to stop, reevaluate, and choose a better course. It's the process of overcoming the obstacles in our lives that allows us to grow.

The first time I learned that lesson I was just three years old. Chasing my brother across the street, I had an encounter with a 1929 Ford that put me in the hospital for two weeks. I believe even at that age, I profited from the setback. From that point on, I had a deeper appreciation for my good life, and a battle-scar on my right temple to remind me I could be as strong as I needed to be to survive.

Family Introduction

I got my hard-headedness from both sides of my family. My mother, Ruth Clump, was an Iowa farm-girl with strong German roots. She grew up understanding that you get what you work for in life, and she was a scrapper right to the end. My father, Harold Cook, had a similar background, with Depression-era values for hard work and thrift. Though my parents were very different in their ways, they were both role models for strength of character and a commitment to working at full capacity.

My mother's family patriarch was her maternal grandfather, Adam Apple. Trained as a cabinetmaker in Bavaria, Germany, he came to America when he was 17 and got his start in life as a gold miner. With the money he made in the gold fields of California, he bought acreage near Beloit, Wisconsin. He and his wife, Dorothea Eckel, raised a family of seven children. Adam served as a Democrat in the Wisconsin state house and senate between 1882 and 1895. When he died at the age of 74, each of the children was left with the equivalent of $10,000 in cash or land.

My mother's paternal grandfather, Frederick Clump, was also German, and came to America with cousins when he was 16. At first he was very poor, living in a sod house with little to eat but ground-squirrels and beans. Once he was established, he married Elmira Mitchell and raised a family on a farm near Superior, Iowa. Frederick was a very spiritual man who taught his children and grandchildren to memorize bible verses and led the local Sunday school. He was a great believer in charity, and after church he always brought someone home to Sunday dinner.

My mother's parents met in Spirit Lake, Iowa, in the late 1800s. Her father, Daniel Clump, was working on a threshing crew, and her mother, Josephine Apple, happened to be among the women who were making meals for the crew. Daniel used to say he fell in love with her because apples were his favorite fruit.

They started their married life on a farm in southeastern Iowa near Clinton. Life there was rugged: my mother remembers rattlesnakes in the hay bales and floods every year. When Grandpa Apple died, my mother's parents used Josephine's share of the inheritance to buy a beautiful farm in the rolling hills near Superior. There was an eight-room house, many outbuildings, a big barn and a cowshed. My mother, Ruth, and her sister, Irene, shared wonderful memories of growing up on that farm.

Ruth Clump met Harold Cook on the campus of Coe College in Cedar Rapids, Iowa, where she was studying to become a teacher. It was the beginning of spring term, and the professor was showing the class the book they would be using. Harold leaned over to the pretty girl sitting in the next row and

2

Daniel and Josephine Clump, Ken's maternal grandparents.

The Cook family circa 1921. Back row: Ruth, Marian, Harold (Ken's father), Donald and Herbert. Standing in front of them: Alfred and Edmund. Seated in the front: DeLoyd Kinnard (D.K.) Cook, DeLoyd Jr., and Esther McKenzie Cook.

told her not to bother buying the book – he'd share his with her. "Right away, I knew he was a Scotchman," Ruth later said.

Harold's family was well educated. His maternal grandfather was a country doctor and his father had a law degree from Drake University, though he had stopped practicing because of the demands of the family farm. Harold's mother was a graduate

of Grinnell College. Harold had dreams of following his grandfather's path as a doctor, but as an undergraduate he was pursuing a degree in education.

In the summer of 1923, Harold bought a new Ford, and he and Ruth decided to drive to Southern California together. They were joined by Ruth's sister, Irene, and her future husband, Graham Harris. Harold and Ruth

Harold Cook *(seated, second from right)* in 1919, when he was editor of his high school annual, the Del Mar Consolidated High School *Pep.*

L: *Ruth's high school graduation photo, taken in 1920.*
R: *an informal photo taken in the same era.*

Ruth Clump and Harold Cook, taken at their graduation from the University of Southern California in 1924.

enrolled in the University of Southern California in Los Angeles and completed their studies there, graduating in 1924. They were married in San Bernardino, California, that same year.

For his medical degree, Harold chose the University of Oregon Medical School in Portland (which later became the Oregon Health & Science University). Ruth got a teaching job in Hillsboro and Harold taught night school, attending medical school during the day.

At that time, housing was very limited in the Marquam Hill area where the university's medical, dental, and nursing programs were taught. When Ruth's father died, she inherited $2,500, which the couple used to purchase a three-story, 12-room home. Harold spent the summer fixing it up, and when it was ready, he and Ruth moved in and started a boarding house for medical students. The house was in a lovely ravine with wild apple trees and blackberries all around. Sometimes the students would shoot pheasants from the back door, and it wasn't uncommon to see deer eating apples in the backyard.

There was an abundance of available building sites in the area, and Harold saw the great potential for constructing badly needed apartments and homes for medical school students and hospital workers. He lost interest in his own schooling, and with limited working capital, became absorbed in the monumental task of developing Marquam Hill. As Ruth cooked and cleaned at the boarding house, Harold kept teaching and doing odd jobs. Every penny they made went toward buying and fixing up more rental properties. At one time they owned more than 100 rental houses and apartments.

The Cook family began to grow when my sister, Marilyn, was born on New Year's Day in 1931. The next child was my brother Richard, who joined the family on the second day of January in 1935.

In the early morning hours of the tenth day of April, 1937, I was born at Wilcox Memorial Hospital in Portland, Oregon, the third child and second son of Harold and Ruth Cook. Baby boy Cook weighed eight pounds, eight ounces and was 21 inches in length, with both head and shoulder

Special delivery: McKenzie Cook and a family friend.

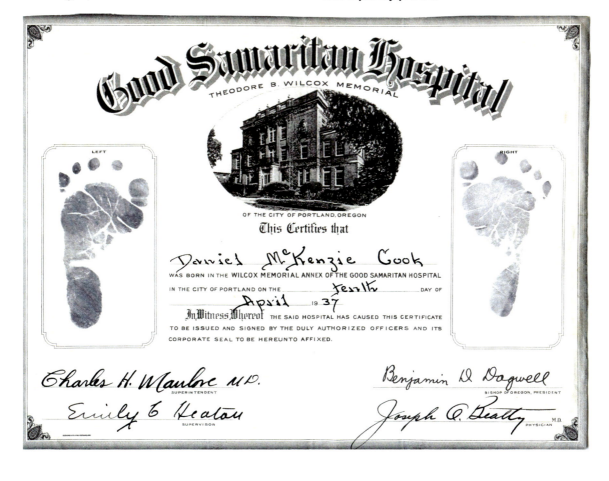

circumferences of 14 inches. The attending physician, Dr. Joseph A. Beatty, reported that I entered the world with "a full set of lungs, lots of energy and an active body." That description still rings true some 75 years later.

A few days after my birth, my parents took me home to Marquam Hill, where they were living at 3333 Veteran's Hospital Road. They had moved about a dozen times in those busy early years, and were currently residing in a place my father had built as a restaurant. The restaurant hadn't succeeded so the family had moved in and rented out half the building to a group of nurses. My mother cooked and served breakfasts and

dinners, boarding-house style. It should be noted that the house is still standing in that same spot today.

On my birth certificate, my name was registered as Daniel McKenzie Cook, which was a tribute to my mother's father, Daniel Clump, and my father's mother, whose last name was McKenzie. However my parents soon reversed those two names and I became McKenzie Daniel Cook. I have been told this name change came about because my mother and father, both being from strong Methodist backgrounds, thought that the shortened version of Daniel, "Dan," sounded too much like "damn." They were perhaps overly concerned that Dan would not be

Marilyn, Richard, and Ruth holding McKenzie at Sellwood Park in Portland.

One Year Old

June 1938 – Brown as a coffee berry.

A Summary of Accomplishments

Walk very well. Began walking at 11 mo.

Climb stairs - can come down steps if watched.

Close doors
Play with my sister and brother
Drink water out of a glass
Pile blocks
Pound with the hammer
Climb up and down from chairs

A Short Sketch of Baby's Characteristics

Baby has blossomed into a darling little boy of 14 months (June). He is very sunshiny and happy disposition - Makes up readily with people. His brown eyes dance with mischief. He cries and shows his stubborn streaks. He's determined and will use force to get his way. (It won't be long before he will take his brother down)

[26]

9

A page from McKenzie's baby book.

well received among their family and friends. I feel there was no harm and therefore no foul in this name change. In fact I think it sounds rather noble! I acquired the nickname "Kenzie" in my very early years, which was shortened to "Ken" as I grew older.

According to my mother's recordings in my baby book, I was a very alert, happy and smiling baby. The second day of September, 1937, was noted as the day my first tooth came through, and by the first of July I had a grand total of 16 teeth. By March of 1938, weighing in at 23 pounds, I was a happy, healthy breast-fed baby who was walking and climbing the stairs.

It's impressive that my mother, with three young children and a boarding house to run, continued to write regularly in my baby book. In mid-1938 she noted that "Baby Kenzie

Big sister Marilyn with McKenzie.

McKenzie with his father, Harold, and sister, Marilyn, circa 1939.

has blossomed into a darling little boy with a strong personality . . . full of smiles with a happy disposition and eyes that dance with mischief." With a mother's insight, she wrote that "Kenzie is stubborn, determined to have his way and not afraid of anything. Baby Kenzie likes to fight with his big brother, Richard, and Kenzie can really take it." I am inclined to believe that Richard and I did have a few "diaper duke-outs" because I vividly remember some of the more vigorous battles we fought as we grew up.

On the third day of August, 1939, my mother gave birth to my little brother, Donn. By this time my sister, Marilyn, was eight, my brother, Richard, was four and I was two. The family was now complete, and my parents both continued to work very hard to provide for us.

My mother, who must have been tired and overworked, was still diligently writing in my baby book. She reported that "Kenzie is a chatterbox, loves to dance with the music on the radio, loves sister Marilyn and baby Donn." On the downside, Kenzie was "still fighting with brother Richard, using newly learned tactics such as biting and pulling hair to make up for the difference in age."

By October 1939, Mother wrote that I had developed into a real worker and loved to help around the house, never stopping until the task was done. "Kenzie loves to play in the dirt, digging with spoons, and likes to ride with his father to the job sites. Harold bought Kenzie a tool chest so that he can hit a 2x4 piece of wood just like his dad, and lets him pick up small pieces of scrap lumber to take home and burn in the fireplace."

In those early years of my life, I was consumed with the love of my parents and my three siblings. Growing up on Marquam Hill, with miles of open space to roam, lush green wooded hills, and fresh clear running creeks, I was living a young boy's dream.

The Accident on Veterans Hospital Road

I've been given many second chances in my life, and I'd like to think I've grown from every one of them. To my mind, a second chance doesn't mean picking up and resuming the same things you were doing when you made your mistake. It means starting over with a new appreciation for where you've been and where you could have wound up, thus becoming a great deal stronger.

My first close call came on the seventh of May, 1940, when I was three years old. That day started like any other, with Mom getting us up for breakfast before starting her housekeeping chores, and Dad leaving to work on a duplex across the street. About midday, I was playing out on the lawn, wearing my "cow-jumped-over-the moon" rubber boots. With my spoon for digging in the dirt and my box of animal crackers, I was completely content. My sister, Marilyn, was close by and my brother Richard was running and playing games with his friends as usual.

I don't remember those minutes just before the accident, but I've been told that I looked up and saw Richard crossing Veterans Hospital Road, dropped my spoon and dashed out after him. Some people say I was run over by the 1929 Ford, and others say I was struck and thrown into a rock wall. In either case, it was not good!

Marilyn started screaming and my father came running from his worksite. He put me in the back of his pickup and headed for Doernbecher Children's Hospital, which was four blocks away. As fate would have it, the head nurse was

Harold Cook holding McKenzie after the accident on Veterans Hospital Road.

12

my Aunt Sara Cook, who ordered that I be taken to surgery immediately. The doctors were summoned for the operation, which lasted five hours. I was kept in the hospital for an additional two weeks of recovery time.

The crash fractured my skull and badly damaged the right side of my face. For years I was plagued by headaches, and doctors have told me the right side of my head is still thicker than the left. But I believe that accident was a blessing in disguise. After my hospitalization, I became more respectful, more caring and more thoughtful. I never ran from a fight and dished out more than I took on the court and playing field. Through adversity, we all become stronger.

Auntie Kellum

After I had fully recovered from my accident, a friend of my mother, whom we called Auntie Kellum, came to visit. She was particularly fond of me, and at the end of her stay, asked if she could take me to her home in Spokane, Washington, to give my mother a little break from her responsibilities. My mother later told me I was proud of my independence and was thrilled to go on the train trip. The visit turned into a six-week stay, which is much longer than my mother had anticipated. Auntie Kellum reported that I never cried and acted like a little man wherever she took me. But although I was a trooper, I was still just a little boy, and when I was finally returned to my home, I ran to my mother's arms, crying, "I just love you, Mommy!"

Richard, age 8, Ken, age 6, and Donn, age 4.

14

The Boys of Marquam Hill

During the years we lived on Marquam Hill, whenever there was an incident in the neighborhood, people immediately assumed that one of the Cook boys was involved. In some cases they were right. Boys will be boys, and in those days it was understood that most boys had to make a little mischief. The world was very different, and children had different kinds of boundaries than they do today.

We roamed the hills by ourselves at a very early age. We never felt at risk, and when the sun went down we were always safely back in the nest. By the time we were five years old, we were deemed responsible enough to have the freedom to come and go as we pleased. We were allowed to take the bus to school in downtown Portland, catch a movie at the Blue Mouse Theater, or cruise the aisles of the Fred Meyer and Meier & Frank department stores. There were only two hard and fast rules we had to promise to obey: Always ask permission and be home before dark.

My brother Richard, being two years older, was both my idol and my rival. He and his friends had a club called the Skull Squad, and I longed to join them. In order to become a member in good standing you had to complete an assignment. Mine was to take my

BB gun and shoot out the lights on the stairs leading up to the Nurses' Residence. Afraid of being seen if I stood too close, I fired from out in the woods, and since I wasn't a very good shot, I didn't have much success. But I did manage to knock out a few bulbs, and for my efforts, I was granted a provisional membership.

Some of the early members of the Skull Squad were Mike Park, Puddy Miller and Vicky Schopper. In today's world we might be called juvenile delinquents, and our parents would be accused of being negligent. But in the 1940s, when children grew up without television, computers, video games or cell phones, we had to use our imaginations to maximize our adventures and exploits in any way we could. Sometimes we got into trouble, but that was just a normal part of growing up.

One of our more colorful escapades was the time we put green dye into Freddie Rogers' watering spring. In those days not every house on Marquam Hill was on the public water and electrical systems, and Freddie was an older man who lived without those utilities. His water source was a spring-fed pool about 200 yards from his house. One day we slipped a big bottle of green food coloring from my mother's cupboard and poured it into Freddie's spring. It didn't do any lasting harm – but it sure shocked him the next time he went down to his watering hole!

Another prank we relished was collecting money from the nurses who crossed the pedestrian footbridge across the canyon. This bridge had been built by the Works Progress Administration in the early 1930s. It was about 300 yards long and rose from the bottom of the canyon to the treetops about 250 feet above the canyon floor. The bridge was made of wooden planks with cracks between them, and if a boy was down below when the nurses were crossing over, he could look right up their skirts! The nurses knew we had a fort under our side of the bridge, so whenever they wanted to cross, they'd yell down "Olly olly oxen free!" and we'd come up and claim a penny toll from each of them.

Ken liked to dress up as Gene Autry, the singing cowboy. He also made good use of his Roy Rogers costume.

We didn't play that kind of prank too often. Most of the time, we just had good, clean fun: sliding down "TB hill" on sheets of cardboard, playing cowboys and Indians with our BB guns, bows, and arrows, running like deer through the lush, damp green woods. The cowboys always won, and when we returned home we were exhausted, hungry and eager to go to bed to dream of yet another day on Marquam Hill.

Above: The gang's first fort, 1940. Ken is on the bottom step and Richard is on the top. Note the footbridge in the background.

Below: Neighborhood kids including Marilyn Cook (back center), Vicky Schopper (back right), Mary Jane Mills (middle left), Puddy Miller (next to her), Bill Park (front left), and Ken with his mother (front right).

Early School Days at Shattuck

From a very early age, I enjoyed my independence. By the time I started kindergarten in the fall of 1941, I was more than ready for the challenge of leaving home. The program was based at Neighborhood House, a community center at the bottom of Marquam Hill. To get there, I walked with my mother one mile to a set of wooden stairs, then walked alone down the 489 steps to the bottom of the hill. My sister, Marilyn, walked me back home at the end of the school day. Today those stairs have been removed to make way for the aerial tram that offers a three-minute ride from the base of the hill to the OHSU campus.

My kindergarten teacher, Mrs. Kelly, was quite an inspiration to me. She always found the positive in every situation. Under her gentle guidance, I learned to cut and paste art projects, draw pictures of animals, say my ABCs and count to 100. To show my fondness for Mrs. Kelly, I would pick flowers for her on my way to school.

After kindergarten, I began attending Shattuck Grammar School in downtown Portland at the south end of the park. It was a two-story red-brick building that had been built in 1915. (Shattuck was later purchased by Portland State University and is now called Shattuck Hall). My brother Richard was two grades ahead of me, and Donn was two years behind me. Marilyn attended Failing Grammar School, which was closer to our home at the time she started school.

Sometime during my third-grade year at Shattuck, my teacher, Miss Prudence Denny, told my mother that I would never make it out of her class. This must have been particularly hard for my mother to hear since she herself was a teacher. Although I can't really remember the circumstances, I somehow learned of their conversation. Once again my determination kicked in and I resolved to prove that Miss Denny was wrong!

The turnaround came in fifth grade, my favorite year at Shattuck. My teacher's name was Mrs. Beutgen, and she set high standards for her students. She was blessed with a passion for teaching and for recognizing the talents of each of her pupils. On my report card, dated the sixth of April, 1948, Mrs. Beutgen wrote, "McKenzie shows initiative and a willingness to study. He has much to contribute, is dependable, and has a nice disposition with very fine work in the fifth grade." On my last report card of the year, I received all C's, which stood for "Commendation" for special effort and achievement. That's right – those C's were the equivalent of straight A's. From then on, although I was never an academic standout, I maintained a respectable grade-point average.

Members of a Shattuck School class display the Indian headdresses they made. Ken is first on the left in the back row. Photo by Angelus Commercial Studio.

It was during my years at Shattuck that I began playing organized sports such as football, basketball and baseball. I excelled in every sport, and when it came to picking a team, I was always chosen first. I loved competition and didn't like to lose. The more it hurt, the harder I would try.

Luckily, my love of sports did not handicap me on the social side of life. I had three girlfriends – Margie Mills, Susan Bedgood and Audrey Owens. I can still remember taking all three out on a "Dutch treat" to the Blue Mouse Theater in downtown Portland. In order to give each girl equal time, I sat between two of them and had the third one sit right behind me so that I could trade off holding hands with them.

Margie Mills was the cutest of the three girls, and she was my favorite girlfriend for a number of other reasons. Her father was a doctor at Veterans Hospital, and they lived on the hospital grounds. Her parents would give me permission to attend the hospital theater, where all the current movies were screened. And best of all, they owned one of the first television sets on the hill.

Looking back, I believe my parents' involvement in school activities had a lot to do with my happy memories of Shattuck Grammar School. My mother was active in the Parent Teacher Association and my dad was always glad to lend his pickup truck toward school projects. In fifth grade, he helped me win the school paper drive, an annual program to collect newspapers for recycling. We would alert people well in advance, and when the time came, I'd go door to door with my Radio Flyer wagon. I'd bundle the newspapers with string and stack them in the garage until it was time to take them to school. I once had two entire walls stacked with papers from floor to ceiling! On weigh-in day, my dad and I would load the papers into his pickup about six feet high and drive down Marquam Hill, with me sitting like a king on top of it all. It's the kind of thing that would never be allowed today! I came close to winning a couple of times, but the year I finally won was a real triumph.

Ken Cook, a tough guy and animal lover.

Name Cook McKenzie
School Shattuck Grade 5

PORTLAND PUBLIC SCHOOLS

PORTLAND, OREGON

GRADES 4 - 8

Name Cook McKenzie
School Shattuck Grade 5

TEACHER'S COMMENTS

Date Nov. 10, 1947

McKenzie contributes much in the field of general knowledge.

Sincerely yours, G. Beutgen

Date Jan. 27, 19__

Shows initiative – Responsible willing worker good work dependable citizen – courteous.

Sincerely yours, G. Beutgen

Date April 6, 1948

Brings in original work. Works up to his capacity. Always active and interested. Nice disposition.

Sincerely yours, G. Beutgen

Date June 16, 1948

Very fine work in the fifth grade

Sincerely yours, G. Beutgen

Pupil Assigned to 6th grade

Ken's 5th grade report card.

Name Cook McKenzie
School Shattuck Grade 5

To Parents:

This pupil progress report is sent home four times a year to inform you of the progress your child is making in the varied activities of the school. All marks are given in terms of the student's own ability to succeed. If he needs special help to progress with his class, you will be invited to confer with his teacher.

You are welcome to call the school for a conference with the teacher or principal for further information about your child.

.... Principal.

EXPLANATION OF MARKS

"C" indicates commendation for special effort and achievement.

"S" indicates satisfactory progress consistent with ability.

"N" indicates need for more effort if progress is to be consistent with ability.

HABITS AND ATTITUDES

	1	2	3	4
1. Accepts responsibility	S	C	C	C
2. Cooperates with others in work and play	S	C	C	C
3. Finds worthwhile work to do independently	C	C	C	C
4. Is courteous and considerate	S	C	C	C
5. Observes school and group rules	S	C	C	C
6. Applies health knowledge to daily habits	S	C	C	C
7. Organizes and completes work	S	C	C	C
8.				

OTHER ACTIVITIES AND SPECIAL ABILITIES

1. ....
2. ....
3. ....

Sept. 1947 to June 1948

	1	2	3	4
ATTENDANCE				
Days Present	47½	41½	44	39
Days Absent	1½	½	½	0
Times Tardy	0	0		0

LANGUAGE ARTS
READING, LISTENING, SPEAKING, WRITING

	1	2	3	4
1. Expresses thoughts well orally	C	C	C	C
2. Expresses thoughts well in writing	C	C	C	C
3. Shows interest in increasingly mature books	C	C	S	C
4. Reads with understanding	C	C	C	C
5. Listens attentively	S	C	C	C
6. Participates in discussion	S	C	C	C
7. Is learning to spell the words he needs	S	C	C	C
8. Writes legibly	S	C	C	C
9.				

SOCIAL STUDIES
HISTORY, GEOGRAPHY, CIVICS

	1	2	3	4
1. Is developing an interest in and understanding of the world about him	C	C	C	C
2. Contributes additional information or material	C	C	C	C
3. Forms judgments based on facts and experiences	S	C	C	C
4.				

ARITHMETIC

	1	2	3	4
1. Shows skill in the use of numbers	S	C	C	C
2. Shows ability to reason in working problems	S	C	C	C
3.				

NATURAL SCIENCE

	1	2	3	4
1. Is developing an interest in and understanding of the world about him	S	C	C	C
2. Forms conclusions based on facts and experiences	S	C	C	C
3.				

ART

	1	2	3	4
1. Shows progress in art expression	S	C	C	C
2.				
3.				

MUSIC

	1	2	3	4
1. Shows progress in music activities	S	C	C	C
2.				
3.				

HOMEMAKING AND INDUSTRIAL ARTS

	1	2	3	4
1. Shows progress in skills				
2.				
3.				

PHYSICAL EDUCATION

	1	2	3	4
1. Shows sense of fair play	S	C	C	C
2. Shows development in individual skills	S	C	C	C

*Ken's first
public speaking
engagement,
Shattuck School,
circa 1948.*

Those were simpler times, and a young boy like me could clearly understand what he needed to do to succeed. When my grades weren't good, I buckled down and did what I could to raise them. When there was a challenge set for collecting newspapers, I made it my goal to be the best newspaper collector in my school. These days, children have so many technical distractions and receive so much information, it must be hard for them to sift through to what's important. I'm glad to have spent my early school years under the strong, clear guidance of Shattuck Grammar School.

Ruth and Ken Cook at a Shattuck School Parent-Teacher Association meeting in 1949. Right: a practice-letter inviting Ruth to a PTA meeting several years earlier.

Portland, Ore.
Nov. 14, 1944

Dear Mother.
Thrusday is P.T.A. meeting. Please come and help us win the prize. Tomorrow is Stamp Day. May I buy a stamp?
Thanksgiving vacation is November 23 and 24
Don't forget P.T.A!
I love you, mother
McKenzie

Successful people lead by example.

The Medical Center Hotel

Marquam Hill circa 1953. Harold Cook built about 75 percent of the buildings in the lower left quadrant of this photo. Veterans Hospital is the flat-roofed building toward the center. The Medical Center Hotel, now the Ronald McDonald House, is the L-shaped building indicated by the white arrow. There was a footbridge between the hotel and the hospital.

In June of 1941, my father completed the construction of the Medical Center Hotel, located at 3340 SW Veterans Hospital Road in Portland. Three stories high, the hotel was perched on the side of the hill next to the wooden pedestrian bridge that spanned the canyon below. It was my father's pride and joy due to its complex construction features, including a concrete walkway bridge that accessed the entrance. The hotel had 35 rooms, and included living quarters for our family on a portion of the upper floor.

The rooms were rented to medical workers as well as family and friends of the patients being treated in the four hospitals: Multnomah County Hospital, Doernbecher Memorial Hospital for Children, Oregon State Tuberculosis Hospital, and Veterans Hospital. All of the hospitals were within a quarter mile of the hotel. The rooms rented for $5 a week or $15 a month, which grossed an income for the family of about $500 per month.

Our family moved into the hotel living quarters in early July of 1941. The spacious living area included a bedroom for my parents and for each of the children. The years we lived there, from 1941 to 1945, were busy and demanding for my parents. My mother had the responsibility of running the hotel as my father constructed homes and apartment buildings all over the hill.

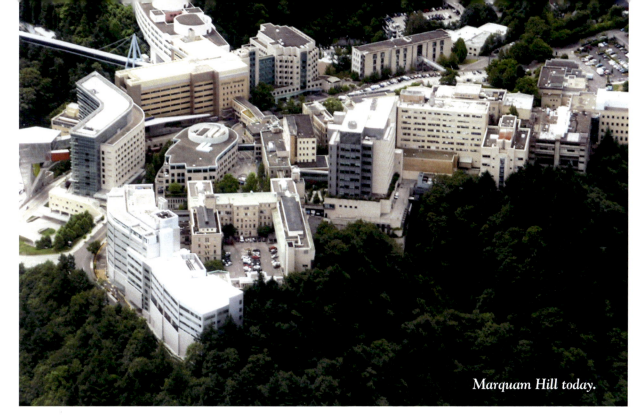

Marquam Hill today.

With the beginning of World War II in early December, 1941, the demands on my parents became even greater. My father was not called into active duty because of his age, marital status, number of children, and also because of his occupation as a builder. But he volunteered to be the Air Raid Marshall for the area, responsible for making sure that everyone complied with the government's wartime mandates. We were required to place blackout curtains on each of the hotel rooms so that no light could be seen from the outside, and each night my father would walk the neighborhood to make sure it was totally dark. Submarines had been spotted off the Oregon coast, and many people feared that the Japanese might attack the mainland.

During the wartime years, my father had a very difficult time securing building materials because they were needed for the war effort. Hardware was especially hard to come by, and I remember one time when my mother had to travel to Denver to buy a case of nails. Because my father did some remodeling work, one of my early jobs was pulling out and straightening used nails from salvaged wood. Somehow, through it all, Dad was able to keep on building.

I honestly don't know how my mother could take care of four children and a husband, cook meals, maintain our living area, and still find time to run the hotel. To make matters worse, the laundry room, minus a dryer, was located on the bottom floor of the hotel – and there was no elevator! She had a remarkable amount of energy, and she didn't slow down until she was well over 60. She always had a smile and a happy, positive attitude no matter how difficult the situation might be.

 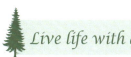 *Live life with a sense of urgency.*

My First Job

My father taught us the value of a dollar, and we learned from his example that it took hard work to earn money. My brother Richard had the first newspaper route on Marquam Hill. He delivered the *Oregonian*, which was the morning paper, to three of the area hospitals.

I learned the tricks of the trade from Richard, and at the age of eight, I too obtained a paper route. I delivered the afternoon paper, the *Oregon Journal*, to the Multnomah County Hospital. I would pick up my 75 papers at the bus stop at the top of the hill, carry them to the hospital, and then walk from ward to ward yelling, "*Journal, Journal*, get your *Journal* right here!" The paper sold for five cents, of which I received one cent for each paper I sold. On a good day I could earn a dollar or more with tips. In 1946, I was named the *Oregon Journal* Junior Boy of the Year and had my picture in the paper. My customers started calling me "OJJ," which made me quite proud.

Delivering the *Journal* taught me a lot of life lessons. The county hospital was for people who couldn't afford Good Samaritan – people at the lowest income level who often didn't have family support and who sadly didn't get the same care as wealthier citizens. Being there every day, I got to know them pretty well and came to understand what a smile could mean to them. I remember bringing gifts to some of my favorite people, flowers or little things I'd made in school, just to cheer up their days.

The county hospital patients were different than the people I saw in my normal life, and they had a profound impact on me. As I made my rounds, I was exposed to psychotic behavior, horrible illness and disfigurement, and sometimes death – things that most children don't learn about until much later in their lives. A large number of the patients were mentally ill and could do cruel things, thinking they were being funny. But I loved my job and learned a lot about forgiveness, humility and patience.

Walking home after finishing my paper route, I would often stop in the neighborhood gift shop and buy my mother a little present. I think that seeing those people in need made me more appreciative of the good things in my own life, especially my family. My mother cherished the trinkets I bought her, and continued to display them in all of her homes.

Oregon Journal *Junior Boy of the Year.*

25

In 1945, my family sold the hotel and moved back to one of our earlier homes at 3416 SW Veterans Hospital Road. My mother, now out of a job, was very happy with the change, having earned a bit of rest. In the summer of 1946, Dad started building our final home in Portland, at 4100 SW 6th Avenue. We moved into that house in the summer of 1947.

To finance some nice furnishings for our new home, my mother enlisted as a substitute teacher for the Portland School District. She substituted at Lincoln, Franklin, Jefferson, Grant and Benson high schools, finding that the pure enjoyment of being back in the classroom was even more satisfying than her paycheck. She gained a new level of self-esteem, and had money to spend as she wished.

By the time we left Marquam Hill in the summer of 1950, my father had built 75 percent of all the houses and apartments in the area. Many of the houses that he sold for $2,500 in the late 1930s are now selling for over $250,000. The true value of the real estate was experienced well after Dad had sold his holdings and had left the area.

The Medical Center Hotel is now a Ronald McDonald House for visiting parents of the children who are patients in the hospitals on Marquam Hill. I enjoy knowing that my mother's love and warmth for the renters of the hotel so many years ago is embodied in the caregivers working there today.

26

A Harold Cook building project on Veterans Hospital Road in 1941.

Marquam Hill Memories

Our last home on Marquam Hill was a futuristic three-story house with 3,000 square feet of living space, built by my father at a cost of over $20,000. My mother was extremely proud of this new home and the years of hard work it represented. The kitchen, dining room, breakfast nook, living room, two bedrooms and a bath were on the main floor. My parents' master bedroom and bath made up the top floor, while Richard and I occupied the two bedrooms on the bottom floor. There was also a furnace room, family room and bathroom on that downstairs level.

For my father's convenience, the home included a two-car garage and an area for his tools and supplies. Our backyard was a forest beckoning us to explore. The Cooks' white stucco house was the talk of Marquam Hill.

Some of the homes Harold Cook constructed are still intact and occupied. Above: Ken and Richard in front of the first house he built. Below: the Hilltop Inn and Restaurant, Ken's first home on Marquam Hill.

For as long as I could remember, our family's only vehicle had been a red and black 1941 Dodge pickup truck. On those rare occasions when we all had to travel together, Mom and Dad would ride in the cab and Marilyn, Richard, Donn and I would sit in the bed of the truck. But Mom didn't like

The Cooks' new home at 4100 SW 6th Ave. was a showplace of modern design in 1947.

the children riding in the back, so our usual mode of transportation was the city bus.

In 1949 Dad decided to buy a new car. He had his heart set on a Ford, a make that was in very short supply in Oregon, so he went off on a shopping trip to San Francisco. When he returned, he was driving a two-door 1949 Ford Business Coupe without a back seat. Mom was so furious with him that I seriously worried she might leave him. Dad knew he had to appease her, and he came up with the idea of building a wooden bench behind the front seat so that at least four out of the six family members could ride together. We were now a two-car family, and despite her anger in the beginning, Mom soon came to appreciate her new freedom. Rather than take the city bus, she could now drive to her teaching assignments, which saved her quite a bit of time.

One of the great delights of our summers was picking wild blackberries. They flourished on every vacant lot on the hill. We would take a couple of our father's used one-gallon leaded paint cans, grab an eight-foot 2x12 plank, and head for the blackberry patch. The best berries were always in the middle of a big, thorny clump. To get to them, we would throw out the plank, stomp it down and walk along the resulting passageway. Richard, whose nickname was Buzz, was renamed Blackberry Buzz for the duration of the season. He was our leader because he had the best technique for throwing the plank, and besides that, he told us he owned the patches! We would come home with a gallon of blackberries and numerous bloody scratches on our arms and legs. After giving our mother the best berries, we would sell the remainder to the neighbors for 25 cents a can. To this day I can still remember the taste of my mother's blackberry pie with vanilla ice cream.

I vividly remember a big fight between Richard and our good pal Vicky Schopper. Forever after it was referred to as "The Main Event," after the old prize-fighting movie. The dispute began when Richard locked himself in Vicky's family car, a new black 1949 Chevy. When Richard finally unlocked the door and let Vicky inside, harsh words were exchanged and Vicky let it be known that he needed to knock some sense into Richard's head. To settle the dispute Richard and Vicky agreed to a boxing/wrestling match in back of Mackenzie Hall, which was part of the University of Oregon Medical School.

All of the neighborhood kids gathered to witness the great match. I feared for Richard because, taking into consideration that I was two years younger, I was faring very well in our brotherly scuffles. At the appointed hour, Richard and Vicky squared off. Vicky danced to his left and Richard danced to his right with fists held high. Vicky motioned for Richard to land the first blow. Richard came from out of nowhere with a strike to Vicky's chin, knocking him off his feet and down to the ground. The fight was over just that quickly, and Richard and Vicky parted friends. With that famous win, Richard became Buzz-Saw Buzz, sealing his reputation as King of the Hill.

Every summer, Marilyn, Richard, Donn and I took our berry-picking talents to the strawberry fields in Gresham, Oregon. We'd start our daily journey at 6 a.m., taking the city bus to Portland where we caught the "strawberry bus" at 7 a.m. Upon arriving at the fields, we were given a flat with nine empty cartons. As each flat was filled, we would take it back to the receiving station for a credit of 25 cents. We could eat all the strawberries we wanted and still go home with some money in our pockets at the end of the day. On a good day we'd make between $1.25 and $1.50 each, a rate of about 20 cents an hour. When the job began to bore us we would throw strawberries at each other. We devised bird names for each of the strawberry field supervisors, and used those names to sound the alert to cover our escapades. "Get to work – Sparrow and Robin heading our way!" It was bliss: having fun, eating berries, and getting paid for it!

Each winter we looked forward to the first snowfall. Marquam Hill was 800 feet above downtown Portland, and occasionally, we could have snow as deep as 12 inches. The bus was not able to make it up the hill, so we would have a snow day, which meant no school. Dragging our sleds, we'd head for TB hill – or get really brave and sled down Veterans Hospital Road to the bottom of the hill. The only problem with that thrilling ride was that at the end, you had to walk over a mile to get back to the top.

Another one of our winter activities was trudging through the woods to cut trees for Richard's Christmas tree business. Donn and I had been well trained: always select a tree over six feet, make sure it is green,

Life is short. If it isn't fun, don't do it.

Christmas of 1947 at the "Marquam Manor."

30

and make a straight, clean cut in order to be able to place a stand on the tree. We would move the trees using our red Radio Flyer wagon. After selecting the best tree for our family, we would sell the rest for 25 to 50 cents each. During a good harvest, we could cut eight to 10 trees and make about three dollars for our efforts. Richard, being the self-appointed expert and banker, would give Donn and me 50 cents each. He would pocket the remaining two dollars, plus change, explaining, "It isn't the pay that you work for – it's the knowledge." I owe my success in the Christmas tree business today to my big brother, Richard.

Christmas was a special time of year for the Cook family. Marilyn would take Richard, Donn and me to downtown Portland to watch the annual Santa Claus Christmas Parade. After the parade we would all go to Meier & Frank and visit Santa Claus, who would give us a candy cane and his assurance that if we were good children, Santa would bring us the gifts that each of us wished to see under the Christmas tree.

Another special treat at Christmas was the radio broadcast of "Judy and Jimmy and the Cinnamon Bear," which aired everyday for the 30 days prior to Christmas. We couldn't wait to get home in the late afternoon to gather around the radio with cups of my mother's hot chocolate and listen to the next episode.

During the summer of 1945, a P-39 Bell Airacobra aircraft crashed near Marquam Hill below Council Crest. The pilot safely bailed out, landing near the hospital. The military quickly sealed off the area, but Richard and I felt that as Skull Squad members, we were obliged to make our own field inspection. Donn saw the no trespassing sign and opted to watch from afar. Our self-assigned mission was to collect a piece of the plane and bring it back for show-and-tell. We accomplished that mission, and as a bonus, we collected several live rounds of 550-caliber ammunition! Being young and naïve, we didn't recognize the danger in playing with live shells. Our secret was soon discovered by our parents and our club's treasure was confiscated.

Today, Richard is one of the few Oregonians who knows exactly where that crash site is located. He intends to revisit the site with a metal detector, searching for more treasure and childhood memories.

My sister, Marilyn, was always there for Richard, Donn and me. She babysat when Mom needed a break, and would tend to our cuts and scratches after our frequent mishaps. Marilyn graduated from Lincoln High School in 1948 and left home to attend Eastern Oregon College of Education in La Grande. When she graduated, Marilyn accepted a teaching position in Madras, Oregon. There she met and married Jack Watts and raised their three children, John, Susan and Alan. Marilyn and Jack still reside in Madras today.

Some of Dad's brothers lived on or near Marquam Hill. Our Uncle Al and Aunt Sara lived on 11th Street in a white house with a view of Mt. Hood. Al was a policeman with the Portland Police Department and Sara worked at Doernbecher Hospital, as I mentioned earlier. We often played with two of their older children, our cousins Alfred and Karen. We all loved Uncle Al and Aunt Sara and thoroughly enjoyed spending time with them.

My Uncle Ed and his wife, Helen, also lived in Portland for a time until they built the Cook's Motel in Brightwood, Oregon, off Highway 26 on the way to Mt. Hood. We usually took a trip to visit Ed and Helen on the Fourth of July to celebrate with fireworks, friendship, and a hamburger and hotdog barbecue.

Other Cook siblings visited from time to time, including Dad's sister Marian Guiberson, who lived in Texas, his brother Herbert Cook from San Bernardino, California, and his youngest brother, DeLoyd Cook, from Denver, Colorado. Once, Richard and I had the great thrill of flying in a DC-3 to San Francisco, where we then boarded a Greyhound bus and traveled on to visit our grandparents in Los Angeles, California. There we enjoyed being surrounded by the Cook clan.

The memories of living on Marquam Hill bring me back at least once a year to walk around the area. Richard and I sometimes go back together, retracing our childhood steps and memories.

D.K. Cook's family, circa 1940. Back row: Herbert Cook, Ed Cook, Al Cook, DeLoyd Cook. Front row: Harold Cook, Esther Cook, D.K. Cook, Marian Guiberson.

Escondido, California, around the time that Ken and his father built the family house. On the left side of the street you can see McCain's Coffee Shop, where they ate breakfast every day.

ESCONDIDO, CALIFORNIA 1951 Heidrick FOTO

One Tough Summer

In early 1949, Mom and Dad made the decision to leave Portland in search of better weather and a more relaxed lifestyle. They selected Escondido, California, a small town 25 miles from San Diego and 20 miles inland from the Pacific Ocean. With a mild climate and only 15 inches of rain per year (as opposed to Portland's 37 inches) it looked like a perfect place to pursue the real estate and building business. For our home, my dad found an ideal lot just two blocks from the high school, a high priority for a family with three boys between the ages of 12 and 16.

At that time, Escondido was a small community of about 5,500 people. Citrus and avocado groves had begun to replace the grape vineyards that had been the town's staple crop since the early part of the century. The name Escondido means "hidden" in Spanish, and the town was considered a treasure in the hidden valley. However by

1950, Escondido had been discovered and was quickly becoming a prosperous full-service city, the business and cultural hub of North San Diego County.

On the first day of July, 1950, Dad and I left Marquam Hill in his red Dodge pickup truck loaded down with tools to build our new home. Why did he take me? Well, Richard was working at the Shell service station, Marilyn was at Eastern Oregon College of Education, and Donn was too young. It was not easy, at 13 years of age, to leave Oregon that summer and head to a new state and a new city without my family and friends. And if I'd known the kind of hard work that was waiting for me in California, I would have been even more hesitant to get into that truck. But there wasn't a choice – this was what my family wanted me to do.

Dad saw this as a great bonding opportunity for the two of us. We would build a house

33

MCKENZIE COOK *Only through adversity do we grow stronger.*

for the family, and we would enjoy our summer together. The first part was true: we did get the house built. But for me, it was *not* an enjoyable summer. The days were hot and the work was grueling. We lived in a motel on the corner of 13th and Escondido Boulevard, away from any social center that might have put me into contact with other kids. I went through my entire summer without meeting a new friend – just sleeping, eating, and laboring at jobs so strenuous they seemed barely humanly possible.

Each day was the same. We would rise at 6 a.m. and drive to McCain's Coffee Shop on Grand Avenue to have breakfast: two eggs, bacon, potatoes, toast, and milk for 35 cents. Yes, that's right, we were both able to eat breakfast for less than a dollar. At 7 a.m. we would arrive at the job site, 409 South Grape, and spend the next 10 hours working. On occasion, Dad would take me with him to Pine Tree Lumber Company to select building supplies, but otherwise the breaks were few and far between. When we got back to the motel at 5:30 p.m., we were tired, dirty, and ready for showers. We had dinner at 6:30, listened to the radio, and went to bed at 8:30. This was my routine six days a week for a total of 10 weeks.

The lot my father had purchased was made of decomposed granite, which had to be broken up and leveled off before we could pour the foundation. We started with picks and shovels, the way my dad had always done it in the soft soil of Oregon. But when it became clear we needed more serious equipment, he went out and rented a compressor and a pavement breaker. I can still remember how loud that machine was when he connected the hose and started the engine. The pavement breaker weighed about 50 pounds, and the hose weighed about 40 pounds. So here I was, a 13-year-old kid weighing in at about 100 pounds myself, lugging a pavement breaker that weighed nearly as much as I did! Up and down the trenches I hauled that thing, wrestling with it to keep it upright as it smashed at the granite. Then I'd use a wheelbarrow to haul the material away. Preparing the lot took about a week and a half, and it was some of the hardest work I've ever done.

On top of it all, I was homesick for Marquam Hill and my Oregon friends. I had my father for company during the week, but often on weekends he'd leave me in the motel and drive down to Los Angeles for a little relaxation. He loved to dance, so he'd spend a night or two at the Biltmore Hotel, where the big bands were playing. At the time I didn't think too much about it, but now it strikes me that he wasn't dancing by himself! Was there anything else going on? I don't think so, but I really don't know. What I do know is that while he was up there having fun, I was stuck in the motel with nowhere to go and no way to get there. In those days, motel rooms were not equipped with a television set, microwave or mini bar. There was a little market nearby where I could buy a few snacks, but nothing in the way of a substantial meal. In that summer of 1950, at the age of 13, I experienced boredom and loneliness for the very first time.

34

A recent photo of the house at 409 S. Grape St., Escondido, California.

After we finished digging the foundation, we poured the concrete, laid the plates, put up the 2x4s, and put the joists and roof on. We did have the help of one other laborer, and my dad hired out the roofing, electrical and plumbing. But otherwise we did all the work to build that house from the ground up. It was awful, but I have to admit that summer left a deep impression on me. When I got older and had a little money, I started building homes myself – one or two a year. I've built about 45 houses and 10 commercial projects during my lifetime.

The finished house was a flat-roofed duplex with a double-car garage in between the two units. Our side had five bedrooms and three baths. The other side had two bedrooms and one bath. Dad had designed the home with a rental unit to pay for the upkeep and taxes on the property. He was always frugal, and

he passed that trait down to me. But he was also very negative, and I've avoided that. He lived through the Great Depression and saw his father go through some pretty serious financial problems. That experience marked him, and he was fond of saying that the next Depression might be right around the corner. "Work hard and save money," he told us. Anything less was "coon-dogging," and there was no worse insult that he could deliver.

Work was everything to my father, and he was a hard taskmaster. His motto was, "a working boy is a better boy." I may have resented it at the time, but I now know that his strictness was a gift. He taught me that hard work is the price you pay for success, and that you can accomplish anything if you're willing to pay that price. I didn't understand it then, but I certainly do today.

If it's good enough, it isn't. Good is never enough when better is expected.

The Family Move to California

In early September of 1950, with the new house almost complete, Dad and I returned to Portland to pack for the family move to California. I was thrilled to be back in Oregon, reunited with my mother and siblings. Two weeks later, just before school started, the family drove to Escondido. We lived in the motel for two months while Dad finished the house, moving in November of 1950.

Our new home was only six blocks from Central Grammar School, where I would spend my eighth grade year. It was there that I met my good buddies Mike Bamber, Frank Woelke and Larry Sjoblem. I also found a new girlfriend, Dixie Bozarth. The class work was much more difficult than at Shattuck, and for the first time in my life I had to really study in order to pass my classes.

In the higher grades at Central, students had a homeroom and different teachers for each subject, which was a new experience for me. I joined the competitive speech class and traveled with the math team, football team and basketball team. I also developed a taste for student government, and looked forward to the many activities I'd enjoy the following years at Escondido Union High School.

As soon as I graduated from eighth grade, Dad and I drove back to Oregon in his red pickup truck to retrieve some items we'd left behind. On the return trip to Escondido, as we were driving down Highway 395 south of Bishop, California, I suddenly felt very ill. By the time we stopped at Lone Pine for the night, I was suffering from extreme nausea, vomiting, and terrible stomach pains. Dad gave me a dose of Serutan, a popular cure-all of the time ("Serutan read backwards spells nature's," was the advertising slogan). During that night I became delirious, and in my agony, ripped the sheets of my bed.

In the morning, with Dad's assurance that I'd feel better soon, we continued on to Escondido. By the time we reached home, I had lost 10 pounds and was as white as a sheet. When my mother quizzed my father about my condition, he gruffly underplayed the whole episode. She insisted on calling our neighbor, Doctor Haley, who ordered me admitted immediately to Palomar Hospital with a ruptured appendix. The doctors told us that if I had not been hospitalized that day, I would have died. Once again, the good Lord was watching over me.

The Cook clan, photographed at the wedding of Marilyn and Jack Watts in 1954.

Back: Helen Cook, Herb Cook, Al Cook, Jack Watts (groom), Harold Cook, Richard Cook, Marian Guiberson, Donn Cook, Al Cook.

Middle: Del Cook, Ken Cook, Sara Cook, Ruth Cook, Marilyn Cook Watts (bride), Allana Cook, DeLoyd Cook Sr.

Front: Marian Cook, Karen Cook, Fred Cook, Sam Guiberson, Candace Cook and Carol Cook.

  Failure is never fatal; but failure to change can be.

Escondido Union High School

The 1950s were a great time to be alive and attending high school. It was an era of simplicity and innocence. We didn't know about drugs, and alcohol didn't have much of a presence in the high school social scene. There may have been a few students who smoked, but they were on the outskirts of the group. Television was just getting started and a lot of times there was literally nothing on, so we weren't consumed by electronics. We did many things as families – kids would come over to my house for dinner, or I'd go to theirs. The mood of the country was upbeat with the memory of our victory in World War II and a strong economic outlook. I can't remember ever feeling a negative vibe during those high school years.

I attended Escondido Union High School, "the school on the hill," established in 1884. It is the second oldest high school in San Diego County, preceded only by San Diego High School. The Escondido Cougars were known throughout San Diego County and mightily feared by all opponents.

In the early 1950s, freshman hazing by the upperclassmen was very common. The freshmen boys and girls were expected to shine the seniors' shoes and perform other menial tasks, and were publicly paddled for no reason, all in the spirit of tradition and good fun.

Each year, with the senior boys supervising, the freshmen boys carried bags of lime to the top of a mountain on the west side of Escondido, where a huge white letter "E" was etched in the mountainside, clearly visible from the town. The lime was spread over the outlined letter to refresh the white color. It was a time-honored tradition, and the hazing we received as freshmen we gave back in kind when we were seniors.

Escondido High School, 1951.

First year at the new high school campus on North Broadway, the Escondido High School ASB candidates for 1954-55. L to R: Ken, Nancy Clements, Larry Cope, Jim Milne, Sherri Martin, Dorothy Havens, Frank Woelke, and Jack McColaugh.

My freshman year in high school was one of personal growth, new friends and new experiences. I set goals early on to be a good student, a great athlete, and a student leader. In the academic and athletic realms, I was supported in those goals by the outstanding faculty and staff of Escondido High School. Mr. Georges, Mr. Hilmer, Mrs. Couts, Mr. McClurkin, Miss Ming, Mr. Quade, and Mr. Ahler were among the gifted, dedicated teachers who nurtured my academic skills through those four years. Coach Quade, Coach Ahler, Coach Duncan, and Coach West helped me hone my skills on the field and court.

I also got a good start on student leadership when I was elected class president that first year at Escondido High School. I played basketball and football on the "B" teams and started dating a girl named Norma Houck, who later married our classmate Bill Birdsell. At one of my football practices, a junior who was a starting guard on the varsity football team took me under his wing to teach me his blocking skills. His name was Bill Bucher and he became my hero, training partner, mentor, and good friend. I give him credit for much of the success I had on the football field.

During my sophomore year I began playing varsity football and basketball. I started at guard on the varsity football team and was named "All-League" as a sophomore. Our football team boasted a record of six wins and three losses. We were led by Don Portis, Bill Birdsell, Bill Bucher, Karl Geise and Stan Nichols.

Jim Ahler was the well-respected coach of our varsity basketball team. I was point guard on the starting five, along with Tom McGetchin, Don Portis, Rich Gehring, and Leon Hartley. I was named First String-All League in the Metro Conference and our team went all the way to the California

Ken was point guard for Escondido's state-ranked basketball team.

Interscholastic Foundation finals, where we lost to Hemet High School.

Despite the demands of athletics, I remained active in student government and public speaking. In the spring of my sophomore year, I ran for student body vice-president and was elected to serve during the 1953-54 academic year. The student body president was Tom McGetchin, who became my mentor and very good friend.

That summer, after passing my California driver's test, I was able to buy a gray 1937 Ford Coupe for $250. My father told me that a car was the worst investment in the world because it always depreciated in value. He was right, of course, but the freedom of having a car made up for any losses. I always parked on the 4th Street hill adjacent to our house, because the Ford needed a rolling jumpstart or a good push to get the engine going.

I spent that summer and the following one working for my Uncle Ed and Aunt Helen at Cook's Motel in Brightwood, Oregon. My job description was to serve as lifeguard for the new pool and to clean the motel rooms. I made about $300 for the summer's work, which was about $30 a week over a 10-week period. This pencils out to about 65 cents an hour. I was too busy to be homesick, but I missed my family and all my pals back in Escondido.

When I returned home for my junior year, I was immediately caught up in the excitement of another great football season.

*The Cook family,
1951. L to R: Harold,
Ken, Marilyn, Donn,
Richard, Ruth.*

The homecoming game against our rival, Oceanside, was always one of the highlights of the school year. The fun started with a pep rally the night before the big game. Students would gather at the school on the hill and form a serpentine parade, winding their way down to the corner of Grand and Broadway, with police clearing the way. There in the center of town, a huge woodpile had been built, with an outhouse at the top, marked with bold letters, "BEAT OCEANSIDE." After a pep talk from the coach, some strong winning words from the team captain and players, and a few energetic performances

It isn't what you say, but rather what you do in life that really counts.

Five Cougars Make All-Loop Team

FIVE ESCONDIDO PLAYERS LANDED BERTHS on The Times-Advocate all-Metro selections. End Rich Gehring, Guard Ken Cook and Back Don Portis were picked on the first team, while Center Stan Nichols and Back Karl Geise were placed on the second team. Pictured above from left to right are: Gehring, Geise, Nichols, Portis and Cook. (Photo by J. Ralph Shidner.)

Above: As a sophomore, Ken was one of five Escondido High School football players chosen by the local newspaper, the Escondido Times-Advocate, for its All-Metro team. Below: Cheerleaders Marilyn Heller, Joan Ransome, Larry Sjoblem, Sue Redmond, and Deanna Myers.

Scenes from the "Beat Oceanside" rally. Top Left: Ken addresses the crowd on behalf of the EHS football team; Above: the bonfire; Bottom: the serpentine.

from the cheerleaders, the bonfire would be lit. With flames jumping over 50 feet in the air, we would dance around the fire in high spirits. This annual ritual was always attended by about 600 enthusiastic students.

That year I was named All-League in both football and basketball. I was beginning to have some college coaches follow my athletic endeavors, and I was excited to think that I might earn a scholarship.

My girlfriend at that time was Sue Redmond. The Redmond family and their business, Golf Craft, had moved to Escondido from Wisconsin. Sue had three sisters, Noreen, Mary and Nancy, and two brothers, Edward and Tom. Their house had a basketball court, and I spent more time at the Redmond house playing basketball and watching college football games than I did at my own house. They were a wonderful, loving and giving family, and even though Sue and I did not continue as high school sweethearts, I will always remember her and her family.

Another one of my very good friends was Marilyn Heller, whose parents, Homer and Helen Heller, owned the Homer Heller Ford dealership in Escondido. They lived on Felicita Hill overlooking the city, and their home was always open to Marilyn's friends with a stocked refrigerator and a warm welcome. The Ford dealership is still owned by the Heller family, and Marilyn and I remain good friends to this day.

Cook (No. 77) makes 9-yard gain against Colton.

From an Escondido High football game program.

During that junior year of high school, I added a new interest to my busy schedule. I became involved in the Campus Crusade for Christ movement. The program was spearheaded by one of our teachers, Ken McClurkin, along with my good friend, fellow student and inspiration, Larry Sjoblem. We did some very effective missionary work and helped a lot students accept Christ into their lives.

Larry Sjoblem, who lived most of his life with only one lung, was loved by everyone. Sadly, he died at the age of 20. I remember giving his eulogy at the First Methodist Church in Escondido, filled with his fellow students, friends and family. I was quite honored to be asked to speak, and can still remember some of my words. "Some people live only a few years and have a tremendous impact, while others can live a lifetime and have no impact at all. In his 20 short years

on Earth, Larry touched our hearts and souls, and I know he is at heaven's gate waiting for our arrival." He was a remarkable friend and had a strong influence on my life.

I enjoyed serving as student body vice-president, and in the spring of 1954, I ran for student body president. My opponent was a smart, talented girl named Nancy Clements who gave me a run for my money. But the "Win with Ken" slogan resonated with the student body, and I won the election.

I had been elected with a campaign promise that I would begin every assembly and student body meeting with a prayer. I kept that promise and it united the school during a very difficult time. Because of overcrowding, the school district had announced plans to build a second high school on North Broadway, three miles from the center of Escondido. Early in the process, an old

Above: High school friends. L to R: Janet Scovil, Larry Sjoblem, Marilyn Heller, Richard Cook, Ken Cook.

L: Ken and Larry Sjoblem.

  Don't wait for things to happen; make things happen.

earthquake-safety report surfaced, claiming that the main building at Escondido High School was unsafe. So on March 15, 1955, the building shut its doors forever, to the great dismay of the loyal students of the school on the hill. For the next two school years, the student body was split. Some took their classes in buildings at the new school site, while others stayed at the old school, taking classes in temporary tents, in the auditorium, and in other "safe" buildings on campus. It was very unsettling for students and faculty alike.

Above: Dedication day for the new valley campus of Escondido High School, 1954. L to R: Robert Hird, president of the Escondido Union High School District school board, Ken as ASB president, and Bud Quade, principal of EHS.

Right: A campaign ribbon from Ken's successful run for student body president.

McKenzie Cook as a high school senior, and Mary Lou McRoberts as a freshman.

As a senior, I was among the students based at the new high school. That school year, 1954-55, I was named captain of both the football and basketball teams. It was at this time that I began to take notice of the head cheerleader, Mary Lou McRoberts, who was a very attractive girl, very smart, with great team spirit. I thought she was beautiful and I respected and admired her but did not make any attempt to pursue her, because she was dating one of the school's star athletes, Phil Adams, who played football, basketball and baseball. It would never have occurred to me that someday Mary Lou McRoberts would become Mrs. McKenzie Cook.

For a second year, I was named All League in both football and basketball, and was voted the school's Outstanding Athlete for 1955. I had scholarship offers from Oregon State, University of Kansas, University of Utah, Boise State and San Diego State. As a native Oregonian, I selected Oregon State in Corvallis, Oregon, which offered me a full-scholarship and also promised to secure a job for me.

Escondido High School's 61st annual graduation exercises were held in Memorial Stadium on the new campus the 15th day of June, 1955. My 190-member class was the first to graduate there. After the ceremony,

The Escondido High School song leaders. L to R: Audrey McGee, Carolyn Hansen, Sue Wilson, Terry Brennan, and Mary Lou McRoberts. Mary Lou's little sister, Margaret Scharnweber, was the mascot.

senior class president Jack McColaugh had us move our tassels in the traditional manner, and I said a sad good-bye to many wonderful friends and teachers. I felt a special appreciation for my student-body cabinet members, Jim Milne, Sherry Martin, and Frank Woelke, and for the great senior-class sportsmen like Jim Billotte, Bill Steward, Bill Sullivan, Don Willis and Pete Young. Standing there with my good friends Frank Woelke, Mike Bamber, Larry Sjoblem, Janet Scovil, Nancy Clements, Jerry Cascioppo, Sue Redmond, Josie D'Agosta, and Marilyn

Heller, I felt a great nostalgia for the very special times we'd spent together.

The next chapter of my life would be much more challenging. I would now leave home, live on my own, find employment, start paying my own bills and taking care of my food and housing. It was as if I was starting over in life at age 18, returning to my roots in Oregon. New opportunities and new challenges awaited me at Oregon State University in Corvallis, Oregon.

Back L to R: Ken Cook, Larry Sjoblem, Jerry Cascioppo, Tom Howard, Wesley Peet.
Front L to R: Alex Lievanos, Dave Weseloh, Jack McColaugh.

Those who matter don't judge me. Those who judge me don't matter.

Freshman Year at Oregon State

After traveling 20 grueling hours on a Greyhound Bus, I arrived in Corvallis, Oregon, on the 20th day of June, 1955. My brother Richard, who attended Oregon State in 1954, was working and taking summer school classes in Corvallis. He met me at the bus and I roomed with him over the summer.

Through the Athletic Department at Oregon State, I was able to obtain a job working for R&J Roofing in Corvallis. My job was being the "tar tender," responsible for melting blocks of tar in the hot kettle and then carrying the molten tar to the roofers. It was a physically demanding and very dangerous job. One football teammate working with me suffered third-degree burns when he stepped through a skylight and the tar bucket spilled over his head and body.

Football practice began on the first of September at Parker Field, where the football team practiced and played our home games. I was one of 120 student athletes vying for a position on the Oregon State freshman football team. The competition was at a much higher level than I had experienced in high school. Keep in mind that most of the freshman football players were the best players in their respective leagues from schools throughout Washington, Oregon and California.

I won the starting right-guard position on offense and was named team captain, which successfully launched my college football career. We played five football games our freshman year and won them all. Led by Paul Lowe, the players on the freshman team were the nucleus of the team that would take Oregon State to the Rose Bowl – without me – in 1957.

Soon after I arrived on campus, I was rushed by the Phi Delta Theta fraternity. I accepted their invitation to become a member and moved into the fraternity house in mid-September of 1955. After a period of initiation and hazing, I became a proud Phi Delt, embracing all that the fraternity stood for. That meant a lifestyle somewhere between the Marquam Hill Skull Squad and *Animal House*, mixing good friends, lots of rowdiness, swearing, drinking and chasing women. It was a far cry from my sheltered life at Escondido High School.

My leadership ambitions were still strong, so I decided to run for freshman class president. When I went to put my name on the ballot at the Student Union, I was told that no student coming from outside the state of Oregon had ever been elected to that post. That sounded like a challenge to me. Again, I campaigned on the promise that I would start all student council meetings with a prayer as a way to strengthen and unite our

McKenzie Cook, OSU freshman.

Frosh vs Rooks -- Parker Stadium, Corvallis, October 21, 1955

1955 OREGON STATE ROOK ROSTER

Coach—Dick Twenge

No.	Name	Pos.	Ht.	Wt.	Age	Hometown
11	Gary Heidrich	WB	5.10	168	22	Klamath Falls
12	Michael Carver	WB	5.8	160	18	Bandon
14	Earnel Durden	WB	5.10	170	18	Los Angeles
16	Duane Marshall	WB	5.10	190	18	St. Helens
22	Jim Brackins	QB	6.0	189	18	Redlands, Cal.
24	Larry Chamberlain	QB	5.6	170	18	Sheridan
25	Jerry Handy	QB	5.9	165	18	Corvallis
33	Clarence (Nub) Beamer	FB	5.11	195	19	Roseburg
35	Harman Smith	FB	5.10	195	19	Willows, Cal.
36	Terry Salisbury	FB	5.10	190	17	Salem
38	Bob Milum	FB	5.10	175	18	Newport Harbor, Cal.
40	Don Gilmore	TB	5.11	183	18	Lancaster, Cal.
44	Paul Lowe	TB	6.0	170	19	Los Angeles
45	Bob Smith	T	6.6	205	17	Portland (Linc.)
47	Tony Arana	TB	5.11	173	18	Vale
48	Jerry Martin	TB	6.2	175	18	Prineville
52	Buz Randall	C	6.1	200	19	Estacada
53	Bob Gerke	C	6.0	208	18	Prineville
55	Joe Wade	C	6.0	185	18	Los Angeles
59	Ken Cook	C	5.10	190	18	Escondido, Cal.
60	Henry Boyd	G	5.9	170	19	Warrenton
61	Walt Koontz	C	5.9	175	17	San Jose, Cal.
62	Gary Lukehart	G	6.0	180	19	Campbell, Cal.
63	Darrell Brackenbrough	WB	5.10	163	24	Wheeler
64	Seraphin Sanchez	G	5.9	200	21	San Francisco
65	Gary Jones	G	5.11	170	18	Corvallis
66	Dennis Brundage	G	5.10	185	18	Roseburg
67	Charles Lindsley	G	5.10	185	18	Portland (Benson)
68	Bill Higley	G	5.8	195	18	Vernonia
69	Jon Blissett	G	5.11	175	18	Seaside
70	Ted Bates	T	6.3	203	19	Los Angeles
71	Jim Peoples	T	6.2	210	18	Butte, Mont.
72	John Schwammel	T	6.0	220	18	San Ramon, Cal.
73	Bob Andrews	G	6.0	198	21	Corvallis
74	Bud Norris	T	6.4	235	25	Forest Grove
75	Walter Baird	G	5.9	170	22	Portland (Benson)
77	Dick Lumenello	T	6.2	240	18	Boston, Mass.
78	Don Campbell	T	6.1	201	17	Bandon
79	Phil Naylor	T	5.9	230	18	Riverside, Cal.
82	Carl Maxwell	E	5.11	180	19	Antioch, Cal.
85	John Clarke	E	5.9	185	18	Independence
86	Bill Davies	E	6.0	165	18	Portland (Cleveland)
87	Malcolm McBride	E	6.2	190	19	Lebanon
88	Bob Biby	E	6.0	195	18	South Gate, Cal.
89	Don Haggerty	E	6.2	180	20	Hollywood, Cal.
90	James Ryley	E	6.1	205	18	Campbell, Cal.
91	Mickey Gray	E	6.1	180	18	Portland (Roosevelt)
92	David Kribs	E	6.1	180	18	Bend
94	Henry Erdwins	T	6.0	225	19	Lebanon
95	Dale Coonse	E	6.0	190	23	Prineville

52

Edward Bussee, treasurer; Lois Breese, secretary; Jan Anderson, vice-president; Mackenzie Cook, president; and Dennis Todd, sergeant at arms.

Oregon State freshman class officers. Ken, the class president, is second from the right.

class. I was elected freshman class president by a margin of 3 to 1, and I kept my promise.

My freshman year had become a thrilling mix of school politics, football, my fraternity, religious activities, and academics. Being young and inexperienced, it never occurred to me that I might be taking on more than I could handle. Far from home and the high expectations of my parents, I began to compromise my values and principles. Football, girls, and the fraternity became my top

Facing page: Oregon State freshman roster for 1955. This is the Oregon State team that went on to play in the Rose Bowl on January 1, 1957 — unfortunately, without Ken. In that bowl game, Oregon State lost to the Iowa Hawkeyes 35-19.

priorities. The classroom, student politics, and religion came in a distant fourth, fifth, and sixth on my list.

This problem came to a head toward the end of my first year at Oregon State. In the late spring of 1956, our fraternity decided to do an off-campus work project at a "home for wayward girls." That was a place where girls who got into trouble were sent to be rehabilitated. Volunteering along with me were my fraternity brothers Wally Koontz, Dean Lampros and George Myers.

Our good intention was to paint the buildings and landscape the grounds. Although we had been strictly warned not to make contact with the girls residing at the home,

Today's preparation determines tomorrow's success.

Phi Delta Theta

due to their unfortunate plight, we couldn't help but make a few friends as we worked. They were desperate for a little fun, and we felt it was practically our duty to help. Together we concocted a plan to return later that night to take them out on the town.

We arrived back at the home at about 7 p.m., jumped over a small fence, met the girls, and left in two cars. Everything went well until we returned to the residence at about 11 p.m. Someone had told the authorities that the girls were missing and the police were there in force to meet us. They didn't arrest us but they said they were obliged to report the incident to the university.

Three days later, we were called before the Dean of Men, who put us through an interrogation leading to an embarrassing confession. He told us we would not be expelled but would be placed on "social probation" until we completed the first semester of our sophomore year. This meant we could attend school but could not take part in any social activities. I had used very poor judgment and made a very costly mistake. My first year at Oregon State ended on a negative note, and although my coaches, teachers, and fraternity brothers all encouraged me to stay, I was ashamed of my actions and felt I no longer wanted or needed to be there.

Wally Koontz, one of my co-conspirators in the girls' home escapade, felt the same. We decided we should start anew by enrolling in Santa Rosa Junior College in Santa Rosa, California. Wally's parents lived in Campbell, California, and he invited me to come and live with him that summer before school started.

The Santa Rosa football coach welcomed us with open arms, saying, "I don't very often see two 'blue chip' athletes show up together." With his encouragement, we both happily enrolled at the college for the fall semester.

Two weeks before football practice was to begin, the coach at Santa Rosa Junior College called to inform me that the junior college near Escondido would not release me to play for a school outside my home district. If I wanted to play football for a junior college, I would have to do so as a "Comet" at Palomar Junior College in San Marcos, California. My plans turned on a dime, and I returned to Escondido to begin the next chapter in my life.

Facing page: Above: Ken is in the back row at the far right of this fraternity photo, next to Dean Lampros and Wally Koontz. Jim Coleman, who sponsored him as a rush candidate, is in the third row at the far right. Jim later married one of the Gallo daughters and is currently co-chairman of Gallo Winery.

Below: The Phi Delta Theta freshman rush class. Ken, Dean and Wally are in the front row on the left.

Palomar College

In the early fall of 1956, I was greeted at Palomar College by the head football coach, Rusty Meyers, who jeered, "You didn't think I was going to let you get away with playing football for Santa Rosa, did you?" He proceeded to inform me that football practice had already started, that my gear would be issued today, and that I should report to practice the next morning at 8 a.m.

After registering for classes, I picked up my practice gear, joined the speech club, met a few teachers, and walked around the campus to familiarize myself with my new surroundings. I had changed from a "fighting Beaver" to a "shooting Comet," and actually found myself happy with this new beginning.

The first day of football practice was a real eye-opener. There were 28 players from seven different high schools in the area. One of them, Neal Curtis, could have played with any college team. Except for him, however, only one or two of the entire assembled group would have been qualified to try out for the Oregon State freshman team. The practices were not structured, the coaches were lax in their discipline, and I could foresee that this was going to be a very long season.

Palomar College played eight games, of which we won three and lost five. The last game of the year was against the top-ranked junior college team in the nation, Antelope Valley Junior College from Lancaster, California, coached by Bob McCutcheon. Their team entered the game with a perfect 8-0 record, enjoying a winning streak of 35 straight games. We gave them a hard-fought game but by the fourth quarter, they had scored 33 unanswered points and when the

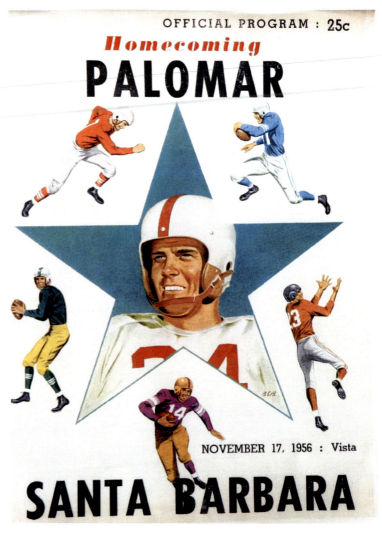

OFFICIAL PROGRAM : 25c

Homecoming

PALOMAR

NOVEMBER 17, 1956 : Vista

SANTA BARBARA

The Palomar College Shooting Comets, 1956. Ken is number 13, front row second from the left.

game ended we were swamped by a score of 40-0. As I was departing the field, Coach McCutcheon walked over to me and asked what my plans were for the following year. I told him that I was considering playing for either Washington State or San Diego State. He replied, "Don't do anything until you hear from me. I'm making a change and I want you to play for me."

I was named the school's Most Outstanding Football Player, First Team All-South Central League, and All-American Honorable Mention Junior College Player. In addition, I was named Palomar College Most Outstanding Athlete of the Year. With these honors came scholarship offers to play for San Diego State, UCLA, Oregon, and Washington State.

That winter, I turned from football to basketball and started at point guard on the Palomar team. Our college did not have a gymnasium on campus so we traveled to the Bing Crosby Hall in Del Mar to practice and play our home games. The basketball team was respectable, and our year ended with a 14-8 record. I was named First Team on the South Central League All-Star Team.

During my days at Palomar, I became reacquainted with Mary Lou McRoberts, who was going to school there after having graduated from Escondido High School in 1956. She was still cheerleading, and she was as smart and good looking as I remembered. However, this time, she was available. We dated for a few months, but when she resumed dating her high school boyfriend, Phil Adams, we parted with some happy memories and a mutual respect.

I ended my days at Palomar with an Associate of Arts degree and honors including Winning Member of the Debate Team and Sportsman of the Year. Most importantly,

If it isn't right with your family, with your parents, and with God, don't do it.

I earned another chance to play football at a higher level. The next chapter of my life was soon to begin with an invitation to play football at the University of San Diego under Coach McCutcheon.

Ken played point guard on the Palomar College basketball team. He is first on the left in the front row. Mary Lou's high school sweetheart, Phil Adams, is in the center of the back row.

Mary Lou McRoberts was head cheerleader in her second year at Palomar College. She competed in numerous beauty contests, and was crowned Citricado College Bowl Queen in 1958.

The University of San Diego

In 1947, Bishop Charles F. Buddy founded the San Diego College for Women, a beautiful Catholic institution on a hilltop overlooking San Diego. In 1954, when a separate College for Men took its place alongside, some dreamed that this small Catholic school might become the West's football equivalent of the University of Notre Dame.

The 1957 University of San Diego football team. Ken is in the second row, last on the right. Dave Cox is in the first row, fourth from the left.

But the school's first football season tempered their hopes. The USD Pioneers, under Coach Gil Kuhn, started their season in the fall of 1956 with a game against the Air Force Academy. The Cadets soared to victory and the Pioneers' lofty dreams were deflated. That first season ended with three wins and six defeats.

I joined the team the very next year, having been offered a full scholarship, including room, books, tuition and a job. For the team's second season, there would be a new coach, Bob McCutcheon (from Antelope

Valley Junior College), new players, a new program, and a strong boosters club.

Since the university was just beginning to expand, there was limited dormitory space. Until other accommodations could be found, new student athletes were housed at the Silver Spray Hotel in Ocean Beach, on the outskirts of San Diego. The football team was called together at the hotel for our first meeting on the last Friday of August, 1957. Thirty-five new players, along with 20 returning players, gathered to make introductions and determine assignments and housing partners. One of the new players, Dave Cox, introduced himself to me and asked if I would like to room with

him. I agreed, and from that meeting came a friendship that lasted more than 50 years, until his death in 2010.

At that same gathering I met another player, Don Gwaltney, a giant of a man who had played on the line for the College of the Pacific in Stockton, California. In conversations with my new teammates, I discovered that most of them had previously attended a four-year college and then left for personal reasons.

Coach McCutcheon had successfully recruited a bunch of hard-nosed football players, and unlike Palomar Junior College, the competition was outstanding. We practiced twice a day at the Marine Base off

From a 1957 San Diego Union story introducing the new season's USD football team.

—San Diego Union Photo by Wayne Badger

Here's the imposing University of San Diego line which will oppose the Barstow Marines tonight at Lane Field when the Pioneers open their 1957 football season. Left end to right are: Merle Reed, Ray Yoast, Ken Cook, Jack Garofono, Don Gilmore, Don Gwaltney and C. G. Walker. Kickoff is at 8:15.

Harbor Drive in San Diego. Our quarterback was Vern Valdez and our star running back was Bobby Keyes, both of whom were Junior College All-American players. That year I also met my good friend Tom Kelly, an outstanding running back whom you will hear more about in later chapters of this book.

I came to camp in the best physical condition of my life. Coach McCutcheon switched me from the guard position to center, and I played that position on offense for the next two years. On defense, I played nose-guard. In the 1950s it was very common for players to play both offense and defense.

Dave Cox and Ken Cook: the start of a long friendship.

PIONEER MULES — Pulling the football wagon for the University of San Diego Pioneers tonight as they open against Bar- stow Marines at Lane Field will be, from left, linemen Dick Gardner (235), Ken Cook (195), John Mulligan (208) and Don Gil- more (182), all newcomers to the Pionee roster. This is the second grid season the University of San Diego.

My friends and I played football, attended classes, dated the girls from the San Diego College for Women, and spent our weekends on Mission Beach. We were getting an education, having more fun than we should, and getting paid at the same time. These were the happy days at the University of San Diego.

Shortly after the football season began, the university rented a large 10-bedroom home in east San Diego for the football players. We lived four to six players per room, and the atmosphere and conditions were truly like an Animal House. I was eager to find other accommodations, and when an opportunity came my way, I took it despite the unusual nature of the place.

The first football game of the University of San Diego's 1957 season aroused a great deal of excitement in the local press.

My new friend Dave Cox had found a job as an apprentice embalmer at the Ryan-Sullivan & Bradley Woolman Mortuary in downtown San Diego. The mortuary was in a large home, and Dave had been invited to live there. He asked me to join him, and after refusing on numerous occasions, I finally relented and accepted a job there as a gardener. Living in a mortuary had its drawbacks from a dating standpoint, but it was a vast improvement over living at the Animal House. Besides, I was living with my good friend Dave, and I had a job that paid me $25 a week.

John Mulligan, center, former University of Colorado and Naval Training Center lineman, and Ken Cook of Palomar Junior College, are a pair of tackles with whom Coach Bob McCutcheon, left,

—San Diego Union Staff Photo

hopes will help University of San Diego obtain a winning season this year. The Pioneers open their second football campaign Saturday night at Lane Field against the Barstow Marines.

The owner of the mortuary, Larry Sullivan, was an avid football fan and gave generously to the university program. He and his family made us feel completely at home. Later in the year, our friend and teammate Don Gwaltney joined us at the mortuary. I soon learned that I could make more money being a mortician than a gardener, so Dave schooled me in the art of embalming and within three months, I was an apprentice embalmer, making $50 a week! (I've devoted the entire next chapter to stories of our mortuary exploits.)

The last two football games of the year were to be played in Mexico City against the University of Mexico and the National Polytechnic Institute. The football team arrived to do battle and we beat the University of Mexico by a score of 38 to 7. Don Gwaltney and I played all 48 minutes of the game, despite the fact that the field was at an elevation of 5,500 feet. When the game was over, Don and I returned to the hotel for a much-needed night of rest and rejuvenation. The rest of the team went out on the town, hitting a local tavern.

Ken and teammate Rick Novack, departing for the USD football team trip to Mexico in 1958.

The next afternoon, Don and I attended a bullfight where we met a young couple staying at our hotel. Later that evening we ran into them at the hotel, and accepted an invitation to join them in their room for drinks. The company was very enjoyable, and we lost track of time until we heard a knock on the door. In walked Coach McCutcheon, who announced that we had missed curfew by several minutes, and had broken training rules by consuming alcohol. Briefly but firmly, he delivered the ultimate blow: "You're off the team." Don reacted furiously, and it was up to me to restrain him as he threatened to throw the coach, who was half his size, out the hotel window.

The following day, Don and I returned to San Diego to face university officials and the press. We took the high road and accepted the responsibility for our behavior. Because

Don Gwaltney and Ken Cook. During the summer months, Don and Ken worked for Bekins Van and Storage in addition to the mortuary. It was hard work but financially rewarding. Between the Bekins and mortuary jobs, they put in 10 hours a day, seven days a week.

  Today's preparation determines tomorrow's success.

of our candor, the university did not take any action against us, and we remained on full-scholarships as students in good standing. We ended that season with eight wins and three loses, which put us in the top 20 Division II teams in the nation.

After the football season ended, I decided to run for student body president. I was elected on a platform advocating that students should have more of a voice in the rules governing the student body. My platform was not too popular with the administration, but the students loved it.

Soon after the election, a harbor cruise was scheduled as a victory party. The boat was jammed with students as well as four or five priests, who were to be our chaperones. A few of the students drank a little too much and the priests drank even more. The following day, the students who drank too much were expelled from school by the same priests who had also been drinking to excess.

As a student leader, I went to the defense of the expelled students. The Dean of Men told me I had a choice: I could also be expelled for insubordination or give up my position as student body president. On the condition that the expelled students would be reinstated in good standing, I resigned my position as president. Through that incident, I learned a lesson: You don't tell a Catholic priest he has contributed to the

COOK-ING UP SOMETHING SPECIAL

Center Ken Cook will pass the ball to quarterback Jan Chapman in Balboa Stadium tonight to start University of San Diego's offense against Montana University. The Thanksgiving feature will start at 7:30 o'clock.

— San Diego Union Staff Photo

This photo accompanied a front-page story in the San Diego Union sports section. Jan Chapman was a dear friend of Ken's.

delinquent behavior of a minor. But I felt that I had maintained my integrity and kept my commitment to the student body that supported me. It was a victory, not a defeat.

In my senior year, I continued to play football for the University of San Diego. Our quarterback, Jan Chapman, led the university to a 7-3 record. Dave Cox was always the opposing quarterback for the scout team, so we gave him the nickname "Big Blue Leader." Because he was originally from Tonkawa, Oklahoma, he also answered to "Okie."

Don Gwaltney and Coach McCutcheon never did make up after Don's attempt on the coach's life in Mexico City. So the best lineman on the team dropped out of the football program and became a sportswriter for the school newspaper. He was, however, able to continue his schooling on a full scholarship earned through his academic and literary skills.

Don married Carol June O'Connor, a University of San Diego student from Chicago. He worked for the Leo Burnett Advertising Agency for many years, and created the well-known "Marlboro Man" advertising campaign. Don is now retired, and the Gwaltneys live in Spring Island, South Carolina. He and I have continued our friendship over the years, and if I were ever asked to assemble a team to go to war, Don would be my first pick.

On a side note, after Don and I graduated from the University of San Diego in June of 1959, we had another chance to play football together. We were both recruited to play for the San Francisco 49ers, but we didn't make the grade and were cut from the team.

During the 1957-58 school year, I dated a girl named Bette Haddad who was from Chicago and attended San Diego College for Women. Bette was a freshman and I was a junior. Because her parents thought we were becoming too serious in our relationship, she did not return to school the next year.

During the school year of 1958-1959, I dated a girl named Judy Bremner, who also attended the San Diego College for Women. Judy was from Skokie, Illinois. Our friendship blossomed into a serious relationship and I traveled to Skokie to meet Judy's parents and ask her father for her hand in marriage. With his approval and blessing, we became engaged in the summer of 1959. We were to be married in the spring of 1960 at the Catholic church in Skokie, with a reception planned for the country club. At the end of her sophomore school year, Judy returned home to finalize the wedding plans and await my arrival later in the year.

However, in the fall of 1959, my life took a dramatic turn. I received a draft notice to report for basic training in the Army. Instead of the Army, I chose to join the Air Force Reserve with my good old pal Donald Gwaltney. I was assigned to fly to San Antonio for basic training at Lackland Air Force Base on January 1, 1960.

Given the uncertainty of my situation, Judy and I agreed that it was best not to be married at this time. After a lot of soul searching, we decided to call off the engagement and go our separate ways. I will always have the utmost respect for Judy and her family, and I am sure today she is happily married with a family of her own.

If it isn't right with you, it can't be right with others.

Ryan-Sullivan & Bradley Woolman Mortuary

Things were never dull during those years we lived and worked at the mortuary. Dave Cox, Don Gwaltney and I performed every job imaginable, and some that were beyond imagining. We picked up the corpses, embalmed them, made funeral arrangements, dressed the corpses, drove the hearse, drove the family car and even provided graveside services when the priest or minister failed to show up. We showed the proper reverence and sobriety when it was required, but behind the scenes, we had a lot of laughs.

The owner of the mortuary, Larry Sullivan, had a drinking problem, and he would hide his bottles in the empty caskets, in caskets that were occupied, in the family car, and in the chapel. It was never easy explaining to a grieving family member why a bottle might have appeared in a very unexpected place. More often than not, the family member would ask for a shot of the whiskey.

One evening Larry told us to take the deceased Mrs. Jones to the chapel for a service and take the deceased Mr. Thomas to the crematory. Don misunderstood the directions and took Mrs. Jones to the crematory and Mr. Thomas to the chapel. As the mourners were filing into the chapel for Mrs. Jones' service, we opened the casket and to our horror discovered that we had the wrong person. I closed the casket, removed it from view, and Dave and I loaded Mr. Thomas into the hearse for a quick trip to the crematory. We got him there just as they were taking Mrs. Jones in to be cremated. The switch was made, and by the grace of God, no harm was done. The services in the

chapel were only slightly delayed and the mourners had no idea what kind of excitement they'd missed.

The families of the deceased would often spend hundreds of dollars to buy fancy new underwear, socks, shoes, shirts, belts, pants and jackets for their loved ones. It was a shame to see that money go to waste: the garments had to be cut up the back in order to be placed on the deceased, and after a brief service, they would never be seen again. Every once in a while, I would notice a new pair of shoes, a belt or a pair of socks on Dave or Don, but I would never ask where it came from. And I admit, once the guys caught me wearing new underwear. Our motto was, "What happens in the mortuary stays in the mortuary." Years later, the city of Las Vegas stole that phrase!

Often we would go to the naval hospital to pick up a corpse only to discover that the legs or arms were detached from the body. Cases like that were beyond the call of duty for lower-level employees, and my good buddy Dave Cox would always handle those pick-ups by himself to shelter Don and me.

We had one unspoken rule at the mortuary. If you came home drunk and made noise, you just might end up in a coffin. I was never so honored, but it happened once or twice to Don and Dave. We could always tell when the offender sobered up: we heard his scream as the top of the casket flew open.

Whenever the clergyman didn't show up for a service, Dave would introduce me as

Reverend Cook and I would perform the ceremony in his place. Dave and I would then split the $50 graveside service fee. The funny thing is, I actually enjoyed the role of part-time minister!

During the summer of 1959, Larry Sullivan hosted the State Mortuary Convention at the Hotel del Coronado on Coronado Island. For entertainment, the group was to be escorted to the Rosarita Beach Hotel in Baja, Mexico, about 20 miles south of the border, for some Las Vegas-style gambling. Larry asked me to drive his limousine with six guests, taking Don Gwaltney as my co-pilot. As we pulled out of the Hotel del Coronado parking lot, Don told me to take a hard left and step on it because we were running behind the other limos. I hooked a left, gunned the accelerator, and then slammed on my brakes as I realized I was about to go over a ledge with a 10-foot drop-off! The limo skidded to a stop, coming to rest with half the chassis hanging out over the edge. If we got out, we might throw off the delicate balance, so we stayed in the car, putting all our weight as far backward as possible. A bystander called a tow truck, and after a very long wait the truck arrived and pulled us back to safety. By then our guests were too rattled to attend the big event, but as it turned out, that was a good thing because the hotel in Rosarita was raided by the Mexican police and arrests were made. The limousine was repaired and Larry Sullivan forgave me. He sent that very same limo to drive Mary Lou and me from the church to the reception on our wedding day.

The Air Force Reserve

Don Gwaltney and I received our Selective Service System draft notices within one week of each other, in the fall of 1959. Don made some calls and discovered there was an Air Force Recruiting Office in Long Beach, California, that had two slots to fill in order to meet its quota for the next group of Air Force Reserve trainees. We immediately headed for Long Beach to sign up.

The Air Force Reserve required only six months of active duty compared to the two years required by the Army. After completing those six months, you were required to attend a once-a-month weekend meeting and a two-week summer camp each year for six years.

We were sent to basic training at Lackland Air Force Base in San Antonio, Texas, where I was selected as platoon leader. After my years of football training, I was well prepared for the rigorous demands of that experience, and I can honestly say I enjoyed it.

It was at Lackland that I met Bobby Bethard, another college football player who in his later life served as general manager of the Washington Redskins, Miami Dolphins, and San Diego Chargers. While we were in basic training, Bobby became very ill with a ruptured appendix, and I spent two weeks caring for my new friend. We have maintained our friendship throughout the years.

After completing basic training, Don and I were reassigned to March Air Force Base in Riverside, California, where we trained as medics, working in the base hospital. My job description included giving shots, sewing up cuts, and providing care for the patients in the hospital.

During our time at March Air Force Base, Don and I would occasionally take women out on the town. On one of those nights, we were in a western-type saloon when two guys came over and started hitting on our dates. A few choice words were exchanged and before I knew what was happening, Don and I were back to back, fighting our way out of the bar. We dished out more than we took, and by the time the police arrived, we'd made it out the back door with our dates in tow.

The next day, Don and I were working at the base clinic when in walked one of the guys we had fought with the night before. He was sporting a black eye and a few cuts under his cheek bone . . . and was neatly dressed in an Air Force first lieutenant's uniform.

We thought we were done for. As the on-duty medics, we were the only ones who could sew up his cuts, so there was no way to avoid him. In our minds, we both reviewed the potential punishments for striking an officer. But by some miracle, he did not seem to recognize either Don or me. He must have been blind drunk that night, and thank heavens for that! His fortunate memory loss allowed us to dodge a bullet.

As I was stitching him up, he told us the story he'd concocted: how on his way home the previous night, he and his friend were jumped by a gang of guys. Don and I expressed our shock at the attack, and praised him for his bravery. Throughout it all, the lieutenant never suspected that the guys who kicked his butt the night before were the same ones who were tending to his wounds the next day.

Every time Don and I are together, we embellish that story a little bit more. There are two times in life when things seem bigger than they really are: when you are very young and when you are very old.

I completed my active-duty service in early June of 1960, and returned to my parents' home in Escondido. I had been offered a teaching position at Escondido High School, subject to completing my secondary teaching credential. To be fully certified, I had to take six more credits, which I intended to complete at San Diego State University the next fall. In the meantime, I would work for my brother Richard, who was constructing a medical building in Escondido at 2nd and Grape streets.

That summer, the stars aligned for the third time, and I was reunited with Mary Lou McRoberts. Perhaps this third time would be the charm.

A playful moment with some of Ken's Air Force Reserve buddies.
Bobby Bethard is next to Ken on the right-hand side of the back row.

A Chance Meeting With Mary Lou McRoberts

Since the last time I'd seen her at Palomar College, Mary Lou McRoberts had boldly embarked on her life's adventures. In the 1950s, a bright young woman had more career options than her mother's generation, but there was still very little encouragement to venture outside traditional fields like teaching, secretarial work and nursing. Most people believed that marriage should be a woman's ultimate career, and the job market consisted largely of entry-level positions that women would take until they were wed.

Mary Lou set her sights on a much sought-after and very exciting profession: air travel. Soon after graduating from Palomar College in 1958, she was selected to begin training as a "jet-age" flight attendant for American Airlines in Dallas, Texas. She hoped to be based in Los Angeles, but after completing six weeks of training, she was instead assigned to Detroit, Michigan.

While she was there, she became engaged to an art director for an ad agency. However, when her long-awaited transfer to Los Angeles finally came through, she was thrilled and anxious to accept it. The engagement and the fiancé did not survive the move.

Once back in southern California, Mary Lou rekindled her romance with her high school sweetheart, Phil Adams. They became engaged and decided to be married as soon as possible. In those days, flight attendants were not allowed to be married, so Mary Lou gave up her job. That proved to be a mistake. She and Phil both had strong feelings about their respective religions, and those differences had caused problems between them in the past. As they got closer to their wedding date, they realized they would never be able to reconcile their beliefs, and they called off the engagement.

Mary Lou was relieved when her supervisor at American Airlines learned of the break-up and asked her to return to her job. Unfortunately, because she had left her job, the airline regulations of that time required her to start training all over again with a class of new flight attendants. The next class was not scheduled to begin for more than six months.

In the interim, Mary Lou returned to her former job in Escondido as an X-ray technician for two orthopedic surgeons, Dr. Alfred Bateman and Dr. Arthur Stanley. As fate would have it, their office was located directly across the street from the medical building I was working on with my brother Richard.

One morning in early June of 1960, I was working on the roof of the medical building when Mary Lou parked her car across from the doctor's office. I noticed her as

Mary Lou McRoberts as a flight attendant for American Airlines.

she walked across the street, and yelled out to her, "Mary Lou McRoberts, where have you been all my life?" Scrambling down the ladder, I was able to intercept her at the corner of 2nd and Grape Streets, where we exchanged a friendly hug and talked briefly. I told her I would give her a call, which I did, and we began dating again the following night.

By the end of July we were seeing each other almost every day. Mary Lou and I were both older and wiser than we'd been when we dated five years earlier, and we began to appreciate each other in a whole new way. We learned that we had the same religious beliefs and wanted the same things out of life. At last, it just seemed right. We were in love, and those summer days were wonderful.

In early August, Richard received a letter from our father's sister, our Aunt Marian, who lived in Dallas. She had a friend,

Antonio Sacconaghi, who was looking for a trustworthy person to manage a gas-line construction project for the city of Detroit Lakes, Minnesota. Richard, who was not available because of his commitment to the medical building, suggested that I take the position. I discussed it with Mary Lou, and we agreed that I should accept the offer. After all, it was just for the balance of the summer and I would be back with Mary Lou in time to attend San Diego State in the fall.

I packed my car and drove to Detroit Lakes, a lovely community that was growing fast as a seasonal vacation destination. There I met with Tony Sacconaghi, the president of Metrocan of Montreal, Canada, and Bob Mitchell, who was managing the gas-line project through Metro U.S. Construction Corporation. Tony put me right to work. From that point on, I was putting in 10 to 12 hours a day, seven days a week, cramming to learn the jargon, nuances and systems of the business.

I really missed Mary Lou and phoned her as often as possible. We wrote to each other every day and I knew in my heart that I wanted to spend the rest of my life with her. It was sometime during this period that Mary Lou gave up the idea of returning to American Airlines because there was no way to guarantee where she might be based, and she was afraid the distance might take a toll on our relationship. During one of my evening calls, I asked Mary Lou to marry me, and she accepted. We set the date for the 21st of January, 1961.

The Detroit Lakes job continued longer than expected, and it was well into the month of December before I was able to return to Escondido. Back together again, Mary Lou and I began to finalize the details of our approaching wedding. Just before we were to be married, we rented a small house that we both liked very much on 11th Street in Escondido.

I was planning to attend San Diego State in the spring semester and start teaching in the fall of 1961. One week before our wedding, I received a telegram from Tony Sacconaghi, who said that I had been named vice-president and general manager of a company now called Metro U. S. Services, and should plan to be in Minneapolis, Minnesota, before the end of January. In that moment, my life plan was altered. After talking with Mary Lou, I accepted the offer and gave up the idea of becoming a teacher. We were never destined to live in that cute little Escondido house, but my new profession opened a whole world of opportunities.

Ken on the Escondido job where he met Mary Lou for the third time in 1960.

A happy wife is a happy life.

Our Wedding Day

The 21st day of January, 1961, was unseasonably warm in Escondido, with temperatures in the high 80s. St. Mary's Church was filled with 200 of our family and friends for the wedding, which was celebrated with a high Mass lasting well over an hour.

Mary Lou was a beautiful bride and I was so very proud of her as I watched her walk down the aisle in her white satin and lace wedding gown. I was nervous about taking the big step, but with Mary Lou at my side, it was very easy to say, "I do."

Dave Cox was my best man, and I later reciprocated when he and Maggie Hargraves were married. Mary Lou's matron of honor was Carolyn Hansen Parrack, whom she had known since the fifth grade. Carolyn and her husband, Gayle, remain our very good friends today.

Fifty years later, the details of our wedding ceremony have faded from my memory. What I do remember is the warmth of the church as we looked out at the smiling faces of our family and friends and were announced for the first time as Mr. and Mrs. McKenzie Cook. The heat was even more pronounced when we stepped through the huge church doors into the sunlight. There, like a cool oasis, was the beautiful black Cadillac limousine that Larry Sullivan had furnished to take us to the reception. Mary Lou had no inkling at that time that the limo was owned by Ryan-Sullivan & Bradley Woolman Mortuary.

Our wedding reception was held at the Escondido Elks Club, where we shared our joy with our family and friends, cut the three-tiered wedding cake and enjoyed a champagne toast. After tossing the garter and throwing the wedding bouquet, we left the reception with rice in our hair and stepped into my 1960 white Ford sedan for our honeymoon in Palm Springs and Big Bear Lake. We could only spend three days before returning to Escondido in order to pack for our road trip to Minnesota, where we would begin our new life together.

Mr. and Mrs.
McKenzie Cook,
January 21, 1961.

Above: The wedding party from L
to R: Carol Cope, Ardie Burrows,
Sue Bucher, Carolyn Parrack,
Dave Cox, Bill Patton, Ray
Yost, Tom Redmond. In front
is Mary Lou's sister, Margaret
Scharnweber, and brother, Ron
McRoberts.

Left: The bride and groom with
matron of honor Carolyn Parrack
and best man Dave Cox.

Left: The wedding reception at the Escondido Elks Club.

Below: Mary Lou's parents, Harry and Lina Scharnweber, and Ken's parents, Ruth and Harold Cook.

Metro U.S. Construction Corporation

After a three-day drive, which Mary Lou and I called our extended honeymoon, we arrived in Detroit Lakes, Minnesota. I had agreed to spend three weeks there, looking in on the job I'd done the preceding summer. We left Detroit Lakes at the end of February and checked into a motel in the St. Louis Park area of Minneapolis, which wound up being our home for the next two months.

Metro U.S. Services was financed by Italy's state-owned oil and gas company, Eni. The Italians were hoping that Metro U.S. Services would give them a way into the lucrative oil and gas market, which at that time was dominated by the "Seven Sisters," a consortium of major oil companies. My boss, Antonio Sacconaghi, was charged with finding utility companies to purchase our services, and he tapped me to help him. As you will read later in this book, Tony Sacconaghi is a member of what I call my "Up-the-Ladder Team" because he had trust and confidence in me, and in my first real job, provided me with an opportunity that was better than most people see in a lifetime.

Tony and I met and agreed to take my car on a two-week trip, visiting utility companies across the Midwest to sell the services of our pipeline utility company. As we proceeded along our tour we were greeted like VIPs, and after two weeks we had secured three jobs. Metro was now a viable company on its way to success. The road trip had gone very well, and I looked forward to getting back to Mary Lou to share my excitement.

But when I returned to Minneapolis, I discovered that Mary Lou, whom I had left alone in the motel room for two weeks without any transportation, was not a happy camper. Prior to our marriage, she had always been able to go where she wanted to go – either by airplane, airport limo, or her own car. Now she had been stuck in a motel room for two weeks with no family or friends to talk to and with very little money. Her days consisted of getting up to catch the hog reports on television, walking over to the Lincoln Delicatessen (where she purchased every one of her meals), and coming back to the motel to stare at the four walls. Before our marriage, any walking she did was through an airport or parking lot. But for the last two weeks, if she wanted to go anywhere, she had to brave Minnesota winter, where if the temperature reached above 10 degrees it was considered to be a fairly pleasant day.

My sincere apologies were accepted, and we agreed to look for an apartment as an initial step toward improving our situation. We had to wait for my first paycheck, but as soon as it arrived, we moved into a furnished apartment in an eight-story building overlooking Lake Hennepin. In general, things improved, but life was still far from ideal, with me traveling three to four days a

Ken with Antonio Sacconaghi,
Detroit Lakes, Minnesota.

  Act as though it were impossible to fail.

On the job for Metro U.S. Construction Corporation in Detroit Lakes, Minnesota.

week and Mary Lou left alone for days at a time without a car. It was around this time that we learned Mary Lou was pregnant and expecting our first child in early November of 1961.

To prepare for our new family member, we rented a furnished house in south Minneapolis, where Tony stored his Rolls Royce in our garage to use when he came to town. I reduced my traveling time and opened an office in downtown Minneapolis. We enjoyed that summer and made some new friends: Larry and Jo Rita Johnson, Mike and Barbara Sill, and Chuck and Nancy Dart.

Our beautiful baby girl, Amy Elizabeth, arrived on the sixth day of November, 1961, and immediately stole our hearts with her dark hair and angelic little face. Of course we thought she was the most beautiful baby we had ever seen. With the birth of our daughter came an increased sense of my responsibilities as a husband and father. My experience in business was limited, and I had to work seven days a week to establish myself in corporate America. As our baby girl grew and thrived, I worked very hard to make the business successful.

In early 1962, Mary Lou and I filed our first joint federal tax return, with a total income for1961 of $5,906.10. A little later in the year, we were surprised to learn that Mary Lou was expecting our second child. We did the math and figured that Amy would be only 16 months old when the new baby was born.

As it turned out, the age difference was even less than that. Thomas McKenzie was born six weeks early on a cold, snowy day, the 21st of February, 1963. The morning of his birth I was driving to Iowa City, Iowa, to meet with the Iowa Southern Gas Company. Mary Lou

Amy Elizabeth Cook.

*Thomas McKenzie
and Amy Elizabeth Cook.*

mother and son were doing fine. When I arrived at the hospital, I went first to Mary Lou and then on to the nursery to visit my new son.

Because he was six weeks early, baby Tommy had no eyelashes or fingernails. Even more surprisingly, he had red hair. I was frankly taken aback when I saw him, and jokingly asked Mary Lou if she was sure that he hadn't been switched with another baby born that morning. She said she was sure he was ours, but agreed he did not resemble his sister and could not explain the red hair! None of those early peculiarities lasted very long. Tom soon began to look like his sister, and over the years, because he was tall for his age, we were often asked if our children were twins.

In 1963, when I paid my federal taxes for 1962, I found that my income had risen to $8,404.40. Never let it be said that I was born with a silver spoon in my mouth! I started at the bottom and worked hard all the way through my career, but never harder than those early years.

had just been to the doctor the day before and was told that the baby would probably be born right on schedule in March. When I arrived at my appointment, I had a message from my secretary, who was taking care of Amy: Mary Lou was in labor and on her way to the hospital.

I was quite worried, and felt I had to get back as soon as possible. Being six hours away from Minneapolis, I decided to drive to the nearby airport and charter a small plane. As we were making our final approach into the Twin Cities, the air-controller in the tower radioed the pilot to let me know that I was the father of a bouncing baby boy, and that

Soon after Tommy was born I found myself traveling throughout the Midwest again to visit job sites and bid on projects. There were also obligations to be met for my Air Force Reserve program, which took me away one weekend each month and for a two-week training camp every summer. Since we still had just the one car, we would load up on groceries before I left for a trip, hoping that we hadn't forgotten something and that the food supply would last until I returned.

When I arrived home from one of my trips, I had the distinct impression that all was not well in the household. After the children were in bed, Mary Lou asked me point-blank if I was happy. When I assured her that I was, I knew what was coming. "Well I'm not. You're an absentee husband, you don't know the children, and they barely recognize their father." It was a long night, but when I awoke the next morning, I realized that she was right and things needed to change.

I told Mary Lou that I would formulate a plan that would take us back to Southern California. On the 19th of May, 1963, I ran an advertisement in the San Diego Union advertising my services under the "jobs wanted" section of the classifieds.

I received five responses. Two were from insurance companies, one was from a plastics company, one was from a construction company and one was from a small equipment-rental company. My only response was to the construction company, and I was hired over the phone by Edward Mendenhall, the president of Arguello Construction in Del Mar, California.

In the summer of 1963, I gave my 30-day written notice to Metro U.S. Construction and began packing for the move back to California. We arrived in San Diego and rented a house at 815 Vanderbilt Place in the Mission Hills area. Then life took one of those abrupt turns. The night before I was to begin my job, Mr. Mendenhall called me to explain that he had been "intellectually dishonest" with me. To save himself from further embarrassment, he was now informing me that the job was no longer available because his company was in serious financial trouble.

When that horrifying bit of information began to sink in, I reached for my briefcase and pulled out the name and phone number of my second choice for employment, the small equipment-rental company. Out of sheer desperation, I immediately called the owner of that company, Rent-It Service, to ask for an appointment.

EXECUTIVE AVAILABLE EXPERIENCED administrator-Construction and related fields; ability proven by past results. Young flexible & untiring. Unlimited capacity for hard work—thrives on responsibility. Take complete charge or work as assistant. Presently employed. Will make initial sacrifices for attractive future. Write: Box W-29, UnionTrib.

Ken's classified ad in the San Diego Union paid off with five responses.

Rent-It Service

A few days later, at 6:30 in the morning, I found myself at the corner of 15th and G streets in downtown San Diego, ready for my 7:00 interview. I was dressed in my best young executive attire, which included a jacket, tie and recently shined dress shoes. At about 6:45, a green 1947 Packard rolled up behind my car, and I watched an elderly man dressed in dark-blue bib overalls emerge. I stepped out of my car and asked if he knew where I might find Gus Kuehler. "You're looking at him," he said, squinting at me. I introduced myself as the young man looking for an opportunity, and he took another moment to size me up. "I don't think you're what I'm looking for," he finally said. In my suit and tie, I must have seemed like an overdressed snob, the kind who wouldn't be willing to start at the bottom, get a little dirty, and put in a hard day's work. Desperate to change his mind, I started telling him my story: a wife and two kids, a job offer that fell through, a solid work ethic and a good, strong back.

Taking pity on me, Mr. Kuehler invited me into the rental dispatch office. After about 30 minutes of my best persuasive skills, he agreed to hire me. Reaching into the closet, he pulled out a pair of overalls. "Go into the bathroom to put them on," he said, "and while you're in there, you can get started on your job by cleaning the toilet." I did exactly what he told me to do that morning as I began training as a yardman, making $1.25 per hour. It was a far cry from my previous position with Metro U.S. Construction, where I was earning a salary of $18,000 per year. But my family was counting on me, and this job was better than nothing.

I worked six days a week, 10 hours a day and learned the equipment-rental business from the ground up. Mr. Kuehler involved me in many of the company decisions, which allowed me a certain measure of pride as the company grew. We updated our rental fleet to include forklifts and backhoes in our large equipment inventory. We introduced the first rental-equipment insurance, which today is standard in the auto and equipment-rental industries. Over the next

88

A recent photo of the first home the Cooks owned, at 3737 Eagle Street, San Diego.

few years, Rent-It Service became the third-largest rental company in the western United States.

In the spring of 1964, with a $4,000 loan from my father, Mary Lou and I were able to purchase a small house at 3737 Eagle Street in the Mission Hills area of San Diego. We paid $28,000 for that house; on a recent visit, we were amazed to learn that the house recently sold for $478,000.

The success of the company allowed me to move up through the ranks, and in 1965, I became the vice-president and general manager, earning $12,000 per year. Gus Kuehler came to me at that time and told me he wanted to retire. Would I would be interested in buying the company?

It was a tough decision, one that would require a sizeable financial risk. My father's advice was, "Don't do it. Save your money." However, I have always believed that when you move in the direction of your dreams, your dreams will become a reality. My dream was to have ownership . . . so I stepped up and made it happen.

In the summer of 1965, I was able to put together a syndication to purchase Rent-It Service for $450,000. The group was made up of four associates from the company: Don Glasrud, Monte Frodsham, Cecil Frodsham, and me. I was to become the president of the new company, which would be called Metro U.S. Services, DBA Rent-It Service. The investor group put in $100,000 and we borrowed $350,000 from Bill Stephens with San Diego Trust and Savings Bank. The former owners, Gus Kuehler and Ernie Dubois, gifted me the equity money I used to purchase their company.

  Destiny is not a matter of chance, it is a matter of choice.

The success of Rent-It Service was due to a few brave souls I want to acknowledge and salute. Jan Bruner was the most competent personal administrator and secretary that I have ever met. Benny Blair was my mentor in the early days, teaching me the contract and dispatch side of the business. "Shorty" Massell, Marv Palmer, Ray Silvers, Bill Temple, Paul Flanagan, Bill Adams, and Larry Woodson were the backbone and the mainstays of Rent-It Service. These were the dedicated men and women who were my associates when I joined the organization. I feel very appreciative to have worked with them to build a great company.

Gus Kuehler provided me with an opportunity to move up in life and experience ownership appreciation. He is a valued member of the McKenzie Cook Up-the-Ladder Team.

Soon after I took over, a good friend and teammate from the University of San Diego, Tom Kelly, phoned me to say he was being transferred to Atlanta – against his wishes. Tom had been a district sales manager for Kraft Foods. With his business skills, warm personality and winning smile, I knew he would be a perfect fit for our company. He became our sales manager and a respected member of our management team. Tom stayed with the company until it was sold, after which he and wife, Pam, purchased a business in Sun Valley, Idaho. We remained good friends and later worked together in another business endeavor.

On the 28th of October, 1965, our family was blessed with our second daughter and third child, Allison Margaret. She was a beautiful baby with big blue eyes, dimpled cheeks, and a very happy disposition. By the time she was four months old, she was absolutely content to sit and watch Amy and Tom at play, and they loved to do silly things to make her laugh.

Not long after the purchase of Rent-It Service was complete, the board of directors approved a plan to expand our company to include rental locations throughout San Diego County, Los Angeles, and Phoenix. The plan was accomplished through acquisitions and start-ups. Between 1965 and 1968, Metro U.S. Services, DBA Rent-It Service became the largest equipment and sales rental company in the United States.

A Wish, a Prayer, a Dream, and a Decision

A wish will change nothing.

A prayer will give you hope.

A dream will move you in the right direction.

A decision will change everything.

Allison Margaret Cook joins the family.
L to R: Tommy, Amy, Mary Lou holding Allison.

Most people miss the right opportunity because
it is dressed in overalls and looks like hard work.

SOMETHING NEW HAS BEEN ADDED TO—

RENT-IT SERVICE

239-2278

CASE 530 CONSTRUCTION KING LOADER-BACKHOE

EXPERIENCED OPERATORS AVAILABLE

From L to R: Ken Cook, Cecil Frodsham, Marv Palmer, John McCann and Dave Glasud. By frequently updating the rental fleet to include the equipment contractors needed most, Rent-It Service developed a large and loyal clientele.

The growth required additional equity, manufacturing and financing, and increased lines of credit. Because of my experience in Minneapolis, where I had a trial-by-fire experience in running a multi-million dollar construction company, I knew a great deal about corporate structure, financing, and how deals are made. So although I was a neophyte when I came into the equipment rental business, I had a solid background in how to work within corporate America.

In the summer of 1967, we built a new home at 1659 Torrance Street overlooking San Diego Bay and the San Diego airport. The total cost of the house was $50,600, and it most recently sold for $1.25 million. Location, location, location: that 3,000 square-foot house with five bedrooms and three-and-a-half baths was five minutes from downtown San Diego.

In the summer of 1968, Metro U.S. Services was approached by Hertz Equipment Rental

FINANCIAL NEWS

Sunday, July 20, 1969   ⑧   **THE SAN DIEGO UNION   B-17**

—Staff Photo by Dan Tichonchuk

Ken Cook, Metro U.S. Services, Inc., president, is shown at the equipment rental firm's headquarters under construction at Aero Drive and Ruffin Road. Over last four years, Metro's volume growth has averaged 75 per cent yearly, of which 25-35 per cent was internally generated, the remainder from acquisitions. Firm ranks No. 2 in its industry.

GROWTH FIRM: METRO U.S. SERVICES

Heavy Equipment Rentals Booming Throughout Area

By CARL PLAIN
The San Diego Union
Assistant Financial Editor

One of the nation's burgeoning business fields and a pace-setting company within it are still relatively unknown nationally.

Yet heavy equipment rental and Metro U.S. Services, Inc., have compiled outstanding performance records. Moreover, they promise sparkling results in years to come.

75 PER CENT RISE

During its last four fiscal years, Metro has achieved sales growth averaging in excess of 75 per cent a year compounded. It now claims No. 2 ranking (next to Hertz Equipment & Rental Corp.) in an industry expected to top $1 billion in revenues for the first time in 1969. Industry volume is increasing more than 25 per cent yearly, and experts figure only one-fourth present potential is being realized.

Metro's president is McKenzie D. (Ken) Cook, 32, who has made a notably successful transition from defensive football player to aggressive businessman. He starred for Escondido High School

and the University of San Diego, and also played a season at Oregon State University and one preseason for the San Francisco '49ers.

WANTED TO COACH

Had he not been injured as an OSU freshman, Cook might still be playing football as a pro linebacker, preparing for the coaching career he dreamed of.

Instead, he now is coaching some 200 employes in the strategies and tactics of business. As in football, he is part of a team.

Cook joined Metro at the bottom of the ladder in June 1963 to start a climb that led quickly to the presidency, and to spectacular company progress.

For fiscal years ended April 30, sales advanced from about $400,000 for 1965 to some $800,000 for 1966, $1.2 million for 1967 and $1.6 million for 1968. Volume for 11-month fiscal 1969 fell just under $3 million. That fiscal year was shortened to coincide with the March 31 yearend of parent Intermark Investing, Inc., which, as Southwestern Capital · Corp., initially invested

$225,000, good for 10 per cent of Metro's equity, in 1968, and increased the holding to 100 per cent earlier this year.

Metro is a star performer for Intermark, a La Jolla conglomerate which makes straight stock-for-stock acquisitions, but offers top managers of subsidiaries incentives in the form of stock "earnout" formulas.

Intermark, Cook says, gives Metro multiple assists, including (1) a vehicle for making acquisitions and (2) enhanced financial capability.

"Ours is a complex industry to finance," he explains, "because it averages about $8 of debt to $1 of equity. We (Metro) have been holding around $5-to-$1 for · the last four years."

LARGE IN FIELD

California gave birth to heavy equipment rental in 1942 when brothers Bill and Bob Grasse of Glendale founded Acme Rentals, now a four-operation company. Then came Rent-It Service, now a Metro division, started here in 1943 with $500 of capital

(Continued or b-19, Col. 1)

Equipment Rentals Are Booming

(Continued from b-17)
apiece by August C. Kuehler and Ernie DuBois.

Today Metro is among the largest of 5,500-plus companies in the heavy equipment rental industry. Metro forecasts sales of $9.44 million for fiscal 1970, and Cook is aiming at $38 million in fiscal 1973.

"Don't bet he won't make it," advises an Intermark official.

In the last three years, Metro has acquired eight rental and sales companies. It now has 15 locations in Southern California, Arizona and Mexico. Cook expects Metro to have 70 rental yards and 10 equipment sales locations in fiscal 1973. He plans to open regional offices in Dallas next year and in Atlanta in 1971.

Extremely rapid growth of his company and industry seems only logical to Cook.

"People are beginning to look into the economics of equipment overship vs. rental," he says. "The key is utilization."

MUCH IDLE TIME

Studies by the Associated General Contractors, he says, incidate that its members use equipment less than 60 per cent of the time. Cook maintains that 68 per cent utilization is the breakeven point. In its own case, he adds, Metro is achieving 78 per cent utilization, and has boosted profits for each of the last four fiscal years.

Rental's advantages to the user, he says, include (1) reducing labor—a major cost—by means of efficient machinery, (2) eliminating the usual capital drain of ownership, (3) obtaining up-to-date equipment engineered for specific needs, (4) avoiding expense of maintenance and repair, both provided by the rental firm, (5) getting free equipment delivery and pick-up service, (6) saving storage space, (7) receiving monthly billings and (8) being able, in the case of contractors, to pinpoint equipment costs. This makes a contingency allowance—sometimes the difference between winning and losing bids—unnecessary.

NOTES CAPITALIZATION

"Owners also have to capitalize equipment," points out Cook. "That has a deficit effect on the balance sheet, reducing borrowing capacity and, hence, bonding capacity."

Further, rental firms provide equipment insurance against fire, theft and damage.

Metro normally turns over its construction and industrial equipment rental fleet in about 30 months, sending some of the withdrawn units to its profitable rental subsidiary in Tijuana. Usually rental fleet equipment is written off over four to six years, and many owners think it starts making them money after that, but "that's when maintenance and repair becomes a big factor," Cook says.

LEASING DIFFERS

Leasing—a big business nationally but a small part of Metro's operation—is a contractual obligation, usually for a year or more. Rental involves no contractual obligation, and often a period of a month or less.

Not everyone is rushing into the rental business because, Cook says, it takes at least a $1 million inventory to get started, business is tied to highly cyclical and seasonal construction, adequate financing is not readily available because many institutions do not understand the reverse debt-to-equity ratios, and the organizational structure is complex.

Metro develops personnel in three-month training programs and gives special classes for people from other companies. It charges non-Metro men $395 for a three-day seminar, limits classes to 25 persons, and presents experts lecturing on systems and procedures, financing, mergers and acquisitions, and personnel-company effectiveness.

MUST SELL CONCEPT

"Our industry is very unsophisticated," says Cook. He reasons that Metro will benefit when the rental concept is developed and sold more effectively across the nation. To that end, he gives numerous talks and time to trade groups.

With Cook as leader, Metro moves as a team. Chairman of the board that sets policy is J. Monte Frodsham, one of the men who bought Metro earlier in the 1970s. Top executives include Al V. Perona, 32, treasurer; Tom V. Kelly, 33, vice president-marketing; Ed C. Stromgren, 43; v.p.-operations, and Ray L. Miller, 35, controller.

Next month Metro will expand from 15th-G Streets downtown to a new 7.5 acre, $750,000 headquarters facility in Daley Industrial Park, Aero Drive and Ruffin Road.

Leased from Daley Corp. for 20 years, the plant includes 25,000 square feet of under-roof space and is regarded by Metro as the industry's most advanced and efficient rental-service-sales center.

93

A recent picture of the home at 1659 Torrance Street, with a view of San Diego Bay.

Company and a La Jolla-based conglomerate called Intermark. Intermark, which was being managed by Nicholas Wallner and Charles "Red" Scott, wanted to acquire Metro U.S. Services. We elected to be acquired on a stock transaction for $8 million, where each of the owners would receive $2 million in stock. Our company became a wholly owned subsidiary of Intermark.

One year later, the American economy and construction industry began a steep decline. In an attempt to save itself, Intermark elected to do a 4-1 reverse stock split that would leave fewer shares outstanding. But because the economy was so bad, the stock price continued to drop, and within one year, my shares of the Intermark stock were worth less than $250,000 – a loss of several million dollars.

Intermark continued to grow our business on debt rather than equity, which in a weak market was not a fundamentally sound business practice. I learned very quickly that to be in debt is to be in danger.

Around that time, I had a near-miss that made me grateful once again for God's protection. My friends know I'm always running late, but I never stand someone up or miss a flight – except for this one time. That day in 1969, I was scheduled to catch a commuter plane to El Centro, California, to visit our rental yard and meet with the store manager. I was behind schedule and to make matters worse, I got caught in bad

Right: Photo from an article in The General Contractor titled, "What's Cooking?"

Below: The Rent-It Service team, breaking ground in 1969. Tom Kelly standing far left, Ken Cook third from right.

Close friends from the Rent-It/Intermark years, enjoying a J.L. Case-sponsored trip to Jamaica. Clockwise from top: Al and Joyce Kish, Don and Harriet Glasrud, Ken and Mary Lou Cook, Dave and Maggie Cox.

traffic on my way to the airport. When my flight took off at 11:20 a.m., I was stuck in my car on the highway. I learned about the accident some hours later. According to the reports, the plane had just barely gotten off the ground when the baggage compartment door opened inadvertently. The pilot tried to correct the problem, but he lost control of the plane and it crashed onto the runway, killing 11 people. I count this as my third escape from death.

On the 26th day of February, 1970, we welcomed our third daughter and fourth child, Caroline Anne, an adorable baby and the first of our children to be born with blonde hair. Baby Caroline came home from the hospital to be greeted by a brother and two sisters who were all suffering from the symptoms of chicken pox! Somehow we managed to keep our sweet little baby away from the other children, who were most eager to see what she looked like. Although she escaped that epidemic, she suffered a severe case of chicken pox later, when she was in eighth grade.

In 1972, Red Scott asked me to become the President of Nurseryland Garden Centers, one of the Intermark family of companies. Some years before, I had hired my good friend Dave Cox to serve as vice president of sales for Metro U.S. Services. Under this new plan, Dave would assume my role as president, using his great skills at motivation and moving people toward the

Caroline Anne Cook,
born February 26, 1970.

Left: Dave Cox as president of Rent-It Service; Above: with his wife, Maggie, at the last Cook-Cox family reunion before his death in 2010.

98

accomplishment of a common goal. He was coming into a very difficult situation due to the economy and the debt structure of the company.

Dave did a remarkable job as president, but because of a bad economy and heavy debt, the company was sold in 1977 to Hawthorne Machinery. In that sale we lost daily contact with some of the most wonderful, committed people anyone could be associated with, including Jan Bruner, Jim French, Larry Honick, Carl Kennedy, Al Kish, Don Madison, John McGann, Steve Quinn, Paul Ekberg, Tom Kelly, Bill Richards, Ben Blair, Pete Clark, Don Glasrud, and Dave Cox. They embodied our management framework: dignity and respect for our associates coupled with strong directional strategy, accountability and reinforcement of the positive.

Dave Cox left San Diego for his new home in Sacramento, where he started a highly successful insurance business in 1988. There he developed an interest in politics. His first elected position was to the Sacramento Municipal Utility District Board, and from there his political career quickly snowballed. He was elected to the County Board of Supervisors in 1992, and went on in 1998 to become a two-term state representative and in 2006, a two-term California state senator.

Dave was an effective, respected and successful statewide Republican legislator. He and his wife, Maggie, have three daughters, Cathleen, Margo, and Sarah. When I said goodbye to Dave for the last time just before he passed away on August 20, 2010, I told him that he was going to be fast-tracked into heaven, and asked him to save a place for me. Our University of San Diego "Big Blue Leader" was my college roommate, best man, business partner, and very best friend. He was and will always be a legend. The Cox family and the Cook family have promised to stay close and continue to share our lives just as we have through the last 50 years. We recently held a Cook-Cox family reunion in Welches, Oregon.

Maggie Cox recently joined Mary Lou and me on a cruise of the Italian Riviera, along with Tom Kelly and his wife, Pam. Together, we have come up with a fitting memorial: the Dave Cox Section, directly behind home plate in the University of San Diego's new baseball stadium, to be dedicated in the spring of 2013. Maggie, Tom Kelly, Jan Chapman, Tim Wilbur and I have committed to raising $100,000 toward the project, in order for the section to be named in Dave's honor. It will be a tribute to all that Dave loved: his family, his friends, his country, baseball, and the University of San Diego.

Nurseryland Garden Centers

During the summer of 1972, I became president of Nurseryland Garden Centers, replacing my good friend, founder of the company Wieland "Butch" Collins, who moved up to become chairman of the board. Between 1972 and 1976, we opened 15 new locations and soon became the second-largest retail nursery chain in the United States.

To assure consistency in the education of our managers, we developed an eight-week training program called the University of Nurseryland Training Center. It was based on the very successful University of Disneyland, developed by a friend named Mike Vance. Mike helped me develop the University of Nurseryland training program, and introduced me to a number of people behind the scenes at Disneyland. I was very impressed by the philosophy of Disneyland management and the way the park was run. With Disney's permission, I hitchhiked on their ideas, expanding on them for my own business and for public speaking engagements.

Nurseryland Garden Centers was blessed with a talented staff. It is always amazing to

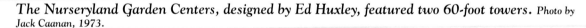

The Nurseryland Garden Centers, designed by Ed Huxley, featured two 60-foot towers. Photo by Jack Caanan, 1973.

A Nurseryland grand opening featuring the company's honeybee mascots. L to R: Red Scott, unidentified, Bill Remmer, Ken Cook, Miss San Diego, Ed Huxley, and Glenna Jones.
Photography by Tally Photography, 1973.

Customer relations mirror employee relations.

Allison and Carey help Ken to welcome visitors. Photography by Tally Photography, 1973.

see what partners and associates can accomplish when they are committed to a goal. The Nurseryland team, consisting of Angel Magana, Tom Ewing, Debbie Ewing, Charles Magana, Bill Remmer, Larry Honick, Bobby Gunnels, Jim Nelson, Jan Bruner, and Butch Collins, created a strong and successful organization with vision, pride, and meaningful results. Ed Huxley was retained as our architect to design our stores for the future. We grew from just three garden centers in 1972 to more than 20 garden centers in 1976, becoming the largest garden center chain in the western United States.

During my time at Nurseryland, I became the television pitchman for the company. With the creative help of Jim Nelson, we made over 50 television commercials. This continued on through my days at the Growing Grounds.

Nurseryland soon became Intermark's largest partner company. This rise to prominence coincided with a movement in America to protect the environment and promote an ecologically healthy approach to our natural resources. Red Scott, the president of Intermark, recognized that movement as an opportunity for Nurseryland to establish itself as a leader in environmentally conscious landscaping. He selected me to became one of the company spokesmen, and after researching the subject, I developed a presentation on corporate stewardship called "Environmental Concern for Today is Caring for Tomorrow." I traveled all over the United States, speaking to corporations, service clubs, and municipal planners.

The Cook family in 1973. Also pictured are Ken's Aunt Marian Guiberson and Uncle Al Cook.

In the spring of 1974, during my brief phase of pilot training, I flew over a very attractive parcel of land near Rancho Santa Fe, California. When I was back on the ground, I drove there and learned that the property was for sale. I purchased a one-acre home site and hired Ed Huxley, Nurseryland's architect, to design a new Cook family home at 37 West Lane in Del Mar, California.

We listed our house on Torrance Street in August of 1976. The first day it was on the market, Mary Lou showed it one time and received an offer of $250,000. We accepted, and moved into our new 3,500 square-foot, five-bedroom, four-bath home in September of 1976. With a swimming pool, tennis and basketball courts, this place made everyone in the family very happy.

Unfortunately, on the business front, things were not going as well. From 1968 to 1976, my Intermark stock dropped from a high of over $3 million to less than $250,000. From that experience I learned a crucial lesson: sell for cash and pay the taxes. Taking stock in the sale of a business is not a safe choice.

I had great respect for Intermark President Red Scott, and went to him to discuss my compensation, stock ownership, and future with the company. In the course of that discussion, I realized that because of my position in the company, I couldn't keep my Intermark stock from losing value, no

Ken and Mary Lou at an Intermark function.

104

The family home in Del Mar had everything the Cooks needed for a comfortable California lifestyle.

Intermark President Charles "Red" Scott.

matter how hard I worked. The only way I could regain control over my net worth was to start working for myself. I made my peace with Red Scott, and resigned from the company. It was not hard saying good bye to Intermark, but it was hard to disassociate myself from a leader like Charles "Red" Scott.

Red Scott will always be remembered for his charismatic personality, oratory skills, energy and creative vision. I consider Red to be a mentor, a valued friend, and an important member of my Up-the-Ladder Team.

High stress and emotional decisions are always wrong.

On the Wings of an Angel

In the spring of 1974, I started taking flying lessons at Montgomery Field north of Mission Valley in San Diego. Ever since I was a young boy, I'd dreamed of learning to fly, and I was finally at a time and place in my life where I could afford to do so.

I was trained to fly in a Piper Cherokee 140. This single-engine aircraft was a two-seater, which only allowed room for the flight instructor and me. After completing 40 hours of flight training, I was able to solo without my instructor. Most of my solo flights were within San Diego County, 25 miles or less from the airport. But for my cross-country solo, I was to fly to Orange County, proceed to Catalina Island, land my plane there and then return to Montgomery Field in San Diego.

My solo flight was scheduled for a beautiful, clear, warm day in August. I mapped my course and started out confidently and without fear. After completing the first leg of the trip, I crossed over Orange County airport at 5,000 feet and proceeded toward Catalina Island for a visual landing. As I approached the airport, which was on top of a cliff at 1,200 feet elevation, I noticed the wind picking up and could see the white caps on the ocean below. I cut back on my power and put my flaps into the landing position.

Just as I was approaching the runway at 1,275 feet, I was hit with the jolt of a down-draft that dropped my plane 100 feet below the top of the cliff. I was moving at 125 miles per hour toward the rocky wall! Without hesitation I banked the plane to the right and went into a steep dive 25 yards from the face of the cliff, heading toward the ocean below me. I applied full power and pulled the stick back just in time to escape crashing into the water.

For a moment, I skimmed across the ocean almost close enough to touch the white caps. As I regained altitude, I realized how near I had come to crashing into the cliff or the ocean, and I thanked God for saving me again. I headed directly back to Montgomery Field without making a second attempt to land on Catalina Island. When I reached the field in San Diego, I went directly to my flight instructor and told him my flying days were over. From that day forward, when taking to the air, I've always been the passenger.

Public Speaking and Consulting

It was at about this time in my career that I began to receive requests for my services as a motivational speaker. Ever since I was a schoolboy, I had enjoyed public speaking, and my environmental presentations for Nurseryland had helped me establish some name-recognition on the speakers' circuit. With a little work, I developed a presentation on my personal business management philosophy, which I called "Mickey Mouse Management." Through my connection to Mike Vance, I was able to get permission from the Disney Corporation to use the famous cartoon character's trademarked name.

When you hear "Mickey Mouse Management," your first thought is that it's going to be fun, and maybe a little off the wall. But this was actually a very serious approach to management. I integrated some of Walt Disney's principles along with some of Vince Lombardi's, and the whole package was pretty catchy. It focused on increased visibility for increased accountability, all leading to a stronger bottom line.

I made this presentation at business meetings and conventions around the country. It was quite profitable and I always had a good time with both the public speaking and the networking afterwards.

Working on the road isn't all fun and games. It has its share of inconveniences, and on one of my speaking trips, I learned just how inconvenient it could be. I had been asked to speak at a bankers' conference in San Francisco. The night before my presentation, I checked into the Saint Francis Hotel and opted to have dinner in my room so that I could watch the World Series, game five. After settling in, I called room service and ordered two scotch and sodas, a shrimp cocktail, and a bowl of soup.

Within 15 minutes, the server was at my door with a rolling cart topped with a white tablecloth and my dinner. She asked if I would like her to place my dinner on the table and I said, "No thank you, just leave the food on the serving cart, it will be easier to move out of the room and into the hall." I undressed and hung up my clothes, and then proceeded to sit on the bed, in the buff, to enjoy my meal and watch the game.

When I had finished my meal, I moved the remainder of my drink to the nightstand and rolled the cart to the door. Because I wasn't dressed, I peeked out into the hallway, looking to the left and then to the right. Just as I pushed the cart through the door and into the hall, the self-closing door hit me in the buttocks and propelled me into the hallway, stark naked. I panicked, pulled the tablecloth off the cart and wrapped it around the most private parts of my body.

My first thought was to find a friendly neighbor who would call security to let me back into my room. I knocked on the door to my right, then to my left, and finally on the door across the hall, but there was no response at any of them. Then I stood at the elevator, hoping a Good Samaritan might get off and help me. I pushed the button and watched the monitor light move toward the tenth floor as if it was on a mission to rescue me. The door opened on an elderly couple, who screamed and began frantically pushing every button on the panel in a desperate attempt to close themselves off from me.

Within two minutes, the elevator was back with a full hotel security force, demanding that I face the wall with my hands in the air. My tablecloth cover dropped to the floor and I was placed in handcuffs.

After a few minutes of questioning, I was able to talk my way out of being arrested as an exhibitionist and possible rapist, convincing the security force I was in fact a guest of the hotel. The head security officer released my handcuffs and gave me a robe. He then escorted me back to my room, let me in with the master key and told me that my meal and drinks were on the house.

The next morning, as I addressed a packed audience of bankers, I shared the story of my hallway capture and subsequent release. When it was over, the entire assembly of bankers stood up and gave me a standing ovation. I was clearly an expert on managing tough situations, and the rest of my presentation was exceptionally well received.

Management Concepts

Mickey Mouse management is based on the visibility of the results. As you increase the visibility of the results (good or bad) you increase the accountability, thus improving the team concept and the bottom-line results. If you don't know the score, you can't play the game. Business is a very serious game that only rewards the winners.

Standards of performance management is the concept of setting acceptable standards of performance by which to manage your business. The "rule of truth" is that the person responsible for the standard must communicate upward before the fact or during the fact — but never after the fact. Based on situations or conditions that change both favorably and unfavorably, standards of performance become the scorecard for business.

Two Chances for Stardom

Through my work as a motivational speaker, I developed an excellent network of highly placed business associates, which led to a number of interesting consulting opportunities. I was considered an up-and-coming entrepreneur with a vision for the future and a powerful motivational message. If truth be told, I had just enough knowledge and experience to be dangerous.

During the early 1970s I had the pleasure of working for two prominent Hollywood businesses. If I had known then the impact these ventures would have on the future of the music and entertainment worlds, I might have extended my involvement with them, but at the time, I saw them both as rungs on my long ladder to success.

I started working with the *Hollywood Reporter*, an entertainment industry trade paper, when it was at a very low point in its long history. Started in 1930, the publication was now under the lead of editor Tichi Wilkerson, and had lost ground to its chief competitor, *Variety*. Its problems centered on cronyism and less-than-factual reporting. Subscriptions, readership and the morale of its employees were at an all-time low. A friend of the editor met me while I was speaking to a group of businessmen at the Biltmore Hotel in downtown Los Angeles, and recommended me as someone who could help turn things around.

This photo was taken when Ken was named San Diego Entrepreneur of the Year in 1978.

In order to understand how the *Hollywood Reporter* was viewed, I decided to interview various Hollywood stars who had been featured in the publication. Through this research, it became clear that three major changes were needed: a new format, more factual reporting on the events taking place in Hollywood, and a bi-monthly, instead of monthly, publication schedule. My team fired people, hired new people, and assured those associates who were performing that

Within each person there are two people: the person you are today and the person you are capable of being tomorrow.

they had a future. The new *Hollywood Reporter* was introduced at a dinner at the home of Francis Ford Coppola in Beverly Hills in the summer of 1976. Mary Lou and I attended the affair, toasted the occasion and thanked our hosts and friends, concluding my one-year consulting assignment.

Over the years, the *Hollywood Reporter* continued to have problems because it was slow to change and modernize. In the fall of 2010 the publication was completely redesigned and re-launched, and currently it is the most respected lifestyle publication in the entertainment world. I'm sure it would exist today with or without my contributions.

Another Hollywood opportunity arose when I was asked to be an advisor and consultant to Barry Gordy Jr., the founder of Motown Records. Gordy had begun producing records under the Motown label in 1959 in Detroit, Michigan. In 1972, he moved his main operations to Los Angeles. All of the famous singers of the 1960s and 70s were under contract with Motown Records. This includes Smokey Robinson, Marvin Gaye, Stevie Wonder, Diana Ross and the Supremes, Martha Reeves, the Jackson 5, and Gladys Knight and the Pips, to name just a few.

Morris Pickus, a good friend and business associate of mine from San Diego, introduced me to Barry Gordy and his Motown

Ken and Mary Lou at a Hollywood function in 1976.

associates. Morris was under contract with Barry to help him build a corporate structure and philosophy.

Not being into that style of music myself, and never having a full appreciation for the artists, I found it very difficult to be of any real value, and my work with Motown ended before it started. In retrospect, I now view this as an opportunity I should have nurtured and capitalized upon. I had two chances for stardom, and though I never embraced the glamorous Hollywood life, I enjoy the memories of those brief encounters.

The Perfect Smile

Sometime during my years as a motivational speaker, I was invited to address the Northern California branch of TEC, a professional development group for CEOs, presidents and business owners. After the meeting, a distinguished Asian gentleman came up to me and introduced himself as Dr. Ben Ichinose, a high-profile orthodontist in the Bay Area. He said he would like to retain me as his personal and business mentor. We exchanged business cards and two weeks later, he invited me to visit his San Francisco offices and meet his associates. We would have dinner and spend the evening at his house in Hillsborough, on three acres directly across from a home owned by the late Bing Crosby.

In the course of my visit, I learned that he operated one of the largest orthodontic practices in California and the third largest in the United States. I was hired to help him expand that business, which I did by improving his marketing and business strategies. We were the first in his industry to advertise orthodontic services with the image of a smiling face. Dr. Ichinose's practice quickly became the largest and most successful in the country. His success was based on three factors: aggressive marketing and advertising, affordable prices, and professional, caring associates. Today, that business model is followed throughout the orthodontic profession.

Among the things that made Dr. Ben Ichinose an unforgettable character was his home wine cellar. It was one of the largest in the United States, and his multi- million dollar wine collection was second to none. It was his custom before dinner to go down into his wine cellar and select a bottle of wine ranging in value from $500 to $5,000 to be consumed with the meal. I like fine wines, but my wine of choice is Trader Joe's special, "two-buck Chuck."

While speaking and networking, I met many outstanding professional men and women who were leaders in their respective industries. It was a fun and rewarding time in my life, sharing my experiences, meeting great people and being handsomely paid for my efforts.

I learned that most people are well grounded, have good ethics and values, work hard and smart, and give back to society. The world also has some real simpletons and marginal characters, and yes, I did meet my share of three dollar bills. But I built my life success in dealing with the hundred dollar bills.

Don't judge yourself by your plans, but by your results.

The Growing Grounds

After leaving Nurseryland, I was ready for a new challenge, and I recognized the perfect opportunity when James Hines came to see me in early 1977. He had recently sold his business, Hines Wholesale Nursery, to Weyerhaeuser, and he expressed an interest in starting a chain of nurseries that could compete with Nurseryland. Jim had some great ideas, and I decided to become his partner. Our chain would be called The Growing Grounds, and it would capitalize on everything we had learned in 50 years of experience with the burgeoning nursery market.

Our concept was to design, build and operate a chain of garden centers that were directed toward the woman, age 25 to 55, whose responsibility it was to prepare food, arrange for a party, and select plants and flowers for her home. We had five departments: Cook's Corner, The Garden Party, The Greenskeeper, and Country Flowers, all within the backdrop of the outside nursery area called The Growing Grounds. Consumers loved our concept, presentation, product spectrum and friendly people.

We brought in a number of top-notch professionals I'd worked with at Nurseryland. Ed Huxley provided architectural services, and Tom Ewing and Bill Remmer brought their nursery skills. Mike Vance of Disneyland helped design an associate training program, and Bill Hirsch, a former Disney merchandiser, joined us as well. After more than a year of planning, we opened our first

It's more than a garden center...

Above: The Growing Grounds sales brochure. Right: A very complimentary story in the trade publication Garden Supply Retailer.

112

Cook "wows" consumers with Disney approach to selling

Garden Supply RETAILER
AUGUST 1979

By Richard W. Chamberlin
Editor

Ken Cook has developed eight 5-department garden centers in the San Diego area using the merchandising magic of Walt Disney combined with the business acumen of a CPA. Cook stages his stores so that the consumer will say "Wow" upon entering. He appeals to her many roles with his party, gourmet and gardening shops. And his merchandising talents help move her through every part of the store . . . and buy.

SHE'S 35 years old and a typical consumer. Her kids call her Mom, her husband calls her Honey and the government calls her Number 4774438. She fulfills many roles.

One of them is the family Gardener. As she drives her station wagon into the parking lot of one of Ken Cook's eight Growing Grounds outlets in San Diego County, she is intent on buying some bedding plants.

But once she passes inside the front door, some of her other roles vividly come to mind.

On her left is the Cook's Corner, a gourmet cooking shop. She assumes the role of the family's Food Preparer. To the right is the Garden Party, a department full of gift wrap, cards and party accessories. She assumes another role, that of the family's Social Director. Straight ahead is the Wishing Well, not a department but a display of cascading greenery accented with color. She assumes the role of the family's Interior Decorator.

Cook feels that today's consumer is ready for a more diversified garden center. So he has created eight identical five-department outlets in southern California, and he has plans for 10 more within the next few years. The entire concept started with a consumer profile.

Cook discovered that his typical customer was a married female between the ages of 25-55, had two children, a household income of $20,000 and lived within four miles of one of his stores. He also discovered that she spends an average of 30 minutes each month shopping in a garden store.

He wanted to lengthen her stay by presenting her with an exciting shopping experience, including a product line that would appeal to her many roles.

Disney

Ken Cook is an innovator, but he also admits he's not above imitation. He has used several of Walt Disney's ideas. "We want our guests (he doesn't use the word customer) to be faced with the same dilemma their children face when they first walk into Disneyland," he said. "The

Carey and Allison loved to visit the Growing Grounds stores with Ken.

Growing Grounds in the spring of 1978 in Del Mar, California.

Over the next two years, we opened eight more retail stores, going head-to-head with Nurseryland Garden Centers in a number of markets. Our concept won the consumer's heart and pocketbook. We began to hear people say, "When you come to San Diego, you must visit the San Diego Zoo, Sea World, and The Growing Grounds."

Torrie Schiller was one of our first managers, and she became very instrumental in merchandising, purchasing, training and management. Tom Ewing and I worked in the areas of quality control, guest relations, and business expansion. Tom became a very well respected figure in the retail and wholesale nursery industry. He and his wife, Debbie, remain our good friends today.

While The Growing Grounds was doing very well with its broad range of products, we decided to try opening specialty stores with just the Cook's Corner products. We opened our first Cook's Corner at San Diego's University Town Center, with excellent results. A second Cook's Corner at Mission Valley Town Center was just as successful. These were gourmet cookware stores, and they came to specialize in coffee products. Before long, we had become the leading distributor of whole coffee beans, a forerunner of the coffee-bar trend we've seen in the last 20 years. By 1983 we had 15 Cook's Corners throughout Southern California and Texas.

Cook-Keig Development

In 1979, while I was operating Cook's Corner and The Growing Grounds, I was introduced to Patrick Keig through a mutual friend. Pat had been one of the principals in Checker Auto Supply of Phoenix, Arizona, which had 250 stores across the Western United States. After one evening together we became very good friends, and a few years later we became business partners, developing commercial real estate projects in San Diego. Pat Keig had a profound impact on my life and is a member of my Up-the-Ladder Team.

The first of our projects was the 35,000 square-foot Private Ledger Building in the Sorrento Valley-Golden Triangle area of San Diego, California. With that project and the ones to follow, we developed and marketed a concept called Equishare, whereby we would allow a tenant the right to take a small equity position in the property in exchange for a long-term lease.

Pat Keig was the kind of partner I respected and enjoyed. He was a seasoned retail veteran and an intelligent businessman with a strong financial statement, who understood the risk and reward of business. Pat's honesty, integrity, wisdom and fairness were his trademarks. He was and always will be an inspiration to me.

I truly value the friendship I had with Pat Keig, who died August 15, 2003. Mary Lou and I continue to maintain our friendship with his wife, Bernita, who lives in Flagstaff and Phoenix, Arizona.

Mary Lou and Ken with Bernita and Pat Keig at the Cooks' 25th wedding anniversary party in January 1986.

Follow the Bouncing Ball

When I was younger, it was all about football and basketball. As I got older and gained a few pounds, I wasn't quite as fast, and my sports changed to racquetball, tennis and golf. Being of a competitive nature, I excelled in all three.

In the early 1970s, racquetball became popular among the younger businessmen in San Diego. It provided a rigorous workout, and I enjoyed the challenge of the sport. I joined the Cuyamaca Club and found time after work to play racquetball five days a week. Dave Cox, Tom Kelly and I would meet in the late afternoon and pound the ball until we were exhausted. A quick steam, a hot shower and a fast drive to Mission Hills brought me home in time for dinner.

As the sport gained momentum, new racquetball courts sprang up all over Southern California. I joined the Atlas Club in Mission Valley in the mid-70s and was introduced to competitive racquetball. Leagues were formed and the elite players soon had a platform along with bragging rights. I became one of the better non-professional players in Southern California. The most important match I ever fought was against the number-one national senior player in the United States. What was to be a "cakewalk" for Mr. Roddefer turned out to be the high-water mark of my racquetball career when I beat him in three straight sets, 21-19, 21-17 and 21-15.

After we moved to Del Mar in the late 70s, we built a tennis court at our home and my sport of choice changed from racquetball to tennis. My son, Tom, and his buddies Ray, Scott and Richie, along with my neighborhood friend Bernie Goott, played tennis almost every day. My claim to fame was beating Bernie Goott in 494 straight sets. I was the home-court champion, intimidating my son and his buddies. My tennis skills brought me three championships at Greater San Diego Sports Association tournaments. One year, the San Diego Friars, a professional tennis team, was invited to our home for a party and tennis exhibition to show our friends how the pros play. We hosted some of the legends of the game including Rod Laver, Cliff Drysdale and Billie Jean King.

When I turned 50, my game of choice changed from tennis to golf. I didn't get serious about the sport until the early 90s, after I built our summer home at the Resort at the Mountain in Welches, Oregon. Although I had played golf once or twice a year in the

70s and 80s, I never broke 100 until 1995. I joined the Mt. Hood Golf Club and started playing two to three days a week. The more I played, the lower my handicap. At one time in 2006, my GHIN handicap was 9.7; today it is closer to 18. Along the way I had a few shots that made me feel like a professional player and kept me coming back for round after round.

The Cooks' 30th anniversary in Hawaii.

While playing with Norm and Linda Osborne at the Rancho Bernardo Country Club on August 31, 1999, I got my first hole in one on the 16th hole. On July 24, 2001, I got my second hole in one on the 18th hole at the Resort at the Mountain, hitting the ball 210 yards. My grandson Andy Delbert witnessed that miracle on the green. My third hole in one came on September 28, 2005, at the Oregon City Country Club. My fourth hole in one came last year at the Resort at the Mountain, where I gave my winnings back to the club by buying drinks for everyone. Along with my four holes in one, I have had five eagles and shot my age once.

My golfing days provided me with a lot of good memories and great friends. Norm Osborne, Jeff Winslow, Gary Bishop, Happy Hottmann, Marv Hollingsworth, Bob Burton and Steve Justus were always up for a game. Of all the balls I have bounced and all the games I have played, golf has been the most challenging and difficult sport to master.

Despite my involvement in sports, as I aged, I found my chest circumference trading places with that of my stomach. The only solution was to start a regimen of push-ups. In the late 60s, 70s, 80s and early 90s, I would do 2,000 to 3,000 push-ups a day in reps of 200 to 300 each. Between 1967 and 1987, I did over 1,000,000 push-ups a year. My all-time annual record was 1,235,000 push-ups in 1985. These days I still make time for 50 to 100 push-ups every day. At the age of 75, I'm proud to be a model for the mental and physical health benefits of an active lifestyle.

Ken and Mary Lou, March 1984.

In the fall of 1980, Frank's Nursery of Detroit, Michigan, contacted us and expressed an interest in acquiring The Growing Grounds. After several months of negotiations, we entered a non-binding letter of intent with Frank's to buy The Growing Grounds for the assumption of the debt, equity, and $1 million in cash.

When news of our negotiations with Frank's reached Red Scott, president of Intermark, he contacted me, asking if he could enter into the bidding process. Intermark's offer was the same as Frank's but the cash consideration was $2 million. Jim Hines and I accepted the Intermark offer and sold the business, dividing the proceeds, and we remain good friends today. Jim is also a member of my Up-the-Ladder Team.

After the sale of The Growing Grounds, I was retained by Intermark on a two-year consulting agreement, which included a non-compete agreement stating that I would not compete at the nursery retail level for a period of five years.

Cook's Corner

After the Growing Grounds was sold, Torrie Schiller stayed on to run the Cook's Corner stores. But within two years, the business crashed and we had to sell at a considerable loss. The story of how that business went from a wildly successful franchise to a terrible financial wreck is a sad one, though not uncommon in the business game. You take risks, and if you do everything right, you get the reward. If you don't, it costs you dearly.

The four original Cook's Corner stores were located in four malls: University Town Center, Mission Valley, South Bay, and Carlsbad. They ranged in size from 900 to 1,200 square feet, and were extremely successful, especially in the coffee category. Given the success of those first stores, we made a decision to offer franchise opportunities in California, Arizona, and Texas. Soon we had more than 20 stores. Our vision was to be just like Williams-Sonoma. We offered a broad range of gourmet kitchen products, and put out slick, expensive catalogues to market them.

Like many businesses that grow very rapidly, we got caught up in the expansion, were overwhelmed, and made some serious strategic errors. The first error was trying to compete with a heavy-hitter like Williams-Sonoma. We soon came to understand that company's success was born of years of experience, and as the new kids on the block, we looked pretty weak when we stood up next to them. The second error was to attempt a mail-order catalog business. Even in a limited market, our seasonal catalogues cost about $50,000 each time we'd produce and distribute them, and we were not getting the kind of returns that would justify an expense like that. The third error was to begin a franchise program. When you franchise, you lose a lot of control, and that can lead to a lot of unhappy partners and unmet financial demands.

The Cook's Corner mail-order business became a liability for the company.

But the biggest mistake we made was neglecting the product that should have been our core business. We put our capital into pots and pans, despite the fact that our success was coming from the coffee category. Fresh coffee beans and good coffee had become our trademark. Norm Osborne and I had traveled to Italy with United Coffee to tour the coffee houses, and we had located an architect and manufacturer who would ship completed "Coffee Kiosks" to us. We were even given the opportunity to buy a fledgling company in Seattle called Starbucks, but we passed on the acquisition. We were spread too thin, and we didn't have the capital required to finance the coffee business.

Cook's Corner could have been a great company. If we had focused our attention on developing a coffee distribution system and a network of coffeehouses, we would have been way ahead of the curve. But failure is an important part of life, part of the growing cycle. Failures are just rungs on the ladder to success.

We learned four vital lessons from the Cook's Corner experience: 1) more is not always better, 2) a little success can be dangerous, 3) focus on one thing at a time, and 4) know your market.

Although Cook's Corner was not a financial success, it did have some very positive outcomes on a personal level. Our first daughter, Amy, went to culinary school and became a chef, evidently through the influence of Cook's Corner and The Growing Grounds. She has a keen eye for design

Norm Osborne, Ken Cook and Rene Jennet on a Cooks Corner/United Coffee buying trip to Germany in the early 80s.

and has had several articles published in national magazines featuring her beautifully decorated Spanish Colonial home. Amy is considered an expert on the Mexican holiday celebrated November 1 of each year, Dia de los Muertos, which translates to Day of the Dead. Don't be fooled by the name – it is actually a lively celebration of life. Amy often hosts a party with festive food and her collection of Dia de los Muertos decorations. Amy Cook Davis is married to Randy Davis and has three children, Noah Eichen, Rachel Eichen, and Samantha Davis.

Our second daughter, Allison, spent a great deal of time at Cook's Corner and The

Carey, Amy, Allison and Mary Lou, early 80s.

Growing Grounds when she was a young girl. As soon as she turned 16, she began to work as a sales and checkout associate, and she was loved and respected by the other associates. From that experience, she developed a passion for retail, and today, she's manager of a high-end store in Escondido's North County Mall. From time to time,

  More is less and less is more.

Allison caters parties and creates wonderful displays of her delicious food and spectacular desserts. Allison Cook Castro is married to Larry Castro and has five children, Andrew Delbert, Tyler Delbert, Makayla Castro, Zack Castro, and Dakota Castro.

Our son, Tom, worked in the Cook's Corner warehouse as a teen, and sometimes drove the delivery truck. During one of his night-time deliveries, the truck broke down on the San Diego 805 freeway. This was before cell phones, and when Tom pulled over on the side of the road, he was completely alone and stranded. Throughout his life, Tom has been very athletic, and at that time was an avid basketball and tennis player. After several unsuccessful attempts to flag down a Good Samaritan, Tom decided to run 20 miles north (in freeway traffic) to our home in Del Mar. Thankfully, his mother and father had no idea of what he was doing until he arrived! Since then, Tom has developed a love of long-distance running, and has participated in numerous marathons, 10Ks, and triathlons. His three children, Kendall, MacKenna, and Tanner, all enjoy watching their father cross the finish line.

Tom Cook as a Torrey Pines High School student, when he worked for Cook's Corner.

The Springtime Growers Partnerships

In the late summer of 1980, Tom Ewing and I, along with Norm Osborne and an attorney from Denver by the name of Malcolm Crawford, set up a series of limited partnerships for high-income investors. The investment required a cash payment along with a personal letter of credit, and allowed the investor a four-to-one tax write-off. We were able to raise $1 million to $2 million per partnership, which enabled us to build the fourth-largest nursery growing operation in the United States, Springtime Growers.

Our growing operation was based in the Del Mar/Torrey Pines area of San Diego. Thanks to Tom Ewing's horticultural skills and the perfect climactic conditions, our plants were superior in quality. The products and company flourished, selling to big-box accounts and the landscape trade.

In 1984, Vista Ventures, a venture-capital company on the East Coast, became interested in our business and made a $4 million investment for an equity position.

The Springtime Growers operation covered about 500 acres in the Del Mar/Torrey Pines area.

Springtime Growers was run on strong management principles that Ken has carried over into all of his subsequent businesses. The "commitment coins" shown here — using the "Just Do It" slogan well before Nike trademarked it — were given to each new employee.

CORPORATE PHILOSOPHY

As associates, each of us will:

1) Strive for professional excellence in the performance of our job.

2) Understand and support the corporate direction.

3) Get the job done — do it now.

4) Provide superior service to all our customers and associates.

5) Be flexible, innovative and responsive to change.

6) Manage human and financial resources wisely.

7) Be a team player, helping others succeed — make it happen.

8) Encourage open communication throughout the corporation.

9) Treat all individuals with dignity and respect.

10) Have pride in and sell Springtime to others.

"Always remember: The consistent fulfillment of a promise or a commitment is the mark of a true professional. Our business success and profitability depend on serving our customers better than anyone else."

PROFESSIONAL MANAGEMENT PRINCIPLES

As associates, each of us will:

1) Provide positive leadership. Be responsible and accountable. Create a strong and successful organization with vision, pride and meaningful results.
2) Stress corporate profitability over volume and size.
3) Achieve, recognize and reward outstanding performance. Do not accept incompetency or poor performance.
4) Plan, organize and communicate effectively. Let your actions speak louder than words.
5) Accept people as the greatest corporate asset. Be visible and accessible to all associates.
6) Communicate openly the vision, goals, problems and successes of the corporation.
7) Teams win. Individuals lose. Consider the goal of the company over individual achievement.
8) Avoid internal politics. We have no time or energy for political infighting.
9) Involve our associates by providing opportunities to contribute.
10) Develop productive associates. Delegate, train and motivate associates to their maximum potential.

"Always remember: The consistent fulfillment of a promise or a commitment is the mark of a true professional. Our business success and profitability depend on serving our customers better than anyone else."

124

IT'S SPRINGTIME

Introducing America's new national nursery . . .

Hi, I'm Ken Cook, Chairman of Springtime!

As America's new national nursery, we have some exciting things to tell you...

Many of our potential customers do not know Springtime. Up until now, we operated in the California, Arizona and Nevada markets. As a relatively small regional nursery, we have learned to build our business on quality and customer satisfaction.

Since our beginning in 1980, Springtime has maintained a standard of excellence in values of quality people, quality products and quality service. In the 90's quality will become the standard by which customers will choose a grower.

We welcome Oregon Garden Products to the Springtime family. We look to the Oregon management team to maintain the same quality, integrity and professionalism which supports our commitment to excellence.

Springtime's Oregon Garden Products

SAN DIEGO COUNTY BUSINESS

His Green Thumb Makes Money Grow

Planter Is on Third Successful Venture in Nursery Business

By BARBARA BRY,
Times Staff Writer

For a man who admits he has never had a green thumb, Ken Cook has prospered from the plant business.

When an equipment-leasing firm he headed was sold in 1970 by Intermark Inc., a San Diego mini-conglomerate, Cook became president of Nurseryland, another Intermark company. (Cook had sold the equipment-leasing company to Intermark in 1968.) In six years, he presided over Nurseryland's growth from three to 19 stores.

Frustrated because he wanted his own company, Cook left Nurseryland in 1976 to start Growing Grounds, which quickly became a competitor of his former employer. Four years later, Intermark purchased Growing Grounds' nine stores from Cook and his partner, Jim Hines, for $1.5 million, merging it into Nurseryland.

This time, however, the company retained Cook on a two-year management contract and had him sign an agreement not to compete against Nurseryland in either California or Arizona for five years.

Undaunted, Cook found a way to get back into the nursery business, this time as a supplier to his former company.

Springtime Growers Group, Cook's new company, is a wholesale grower, selling its plants, trees, shrubs and flowers to more than 300 customers including retailers such as Nurseryland, as well as landscape architects and other commercial accounts.

Springtime, which has 125 acres in North San Diego County, planted its first seeds in November, 1980, and started selling plants the following year.

Sales Double

For 1983, Cook expects sales to reach $3 million, or double the $1.5 million last year. In addition, three retail stores called Springtime Gardens should generate an additional $2 million in sales, he said. The

Ken Cook holds a bougainvillea grown by his new company, Springtime Growers Group, which wholesales plants to retail nurseries.   Photos by BOB GRIESER / Los Angeles Times

stores are in Nevada, outside the area specified in the agreement with Nurseryland. Part of the reason for the doubling in sales is that many plants require a nine- to 18-month lead time before they are ready to be sold.

"This is one of the strongest markets in the country," Cook said, explaining the decision to start Springtime. Further, he said, there are only a few large growers in the area. They include Amfac Nurseries California (part of the Honolulu-based conglomerate), which operates a 280-acre wholesale nursery in Rainbow, and Evergreen Nursery in Del Mar.

To satisfy many of their needs, San Diego retailers and landscape architects must buy from growers in Orange and Los Angeles counties, said the husky, suntanned executive who feels most comfortable in blue jeans and boots.

As a full-service grower, Springtime is able to supply trees such as elms and sycamores; "color" such as begonias and marigolds, and ornamentals such as honeysuckle.

Also, Springtime is becoming more active in what is known as "contract growing" in which large users can pick out their plants six to nine months ahead of time. That section is then "tied off" and reserved.

The Intercontinental Hotel, for example, which is being built downtown, has already chosen its plants, Cook said.

Sales to Retailers

For this year, about 60% of Springtime's sales will be to retailers such as Nurseryland and Target. The other 40% will be to landscape architects and major commercial accounts such as the Rancho del Oro Industrial Park in Oceanside and the new housing developments in Del

Mar Highlands, formerly known as North City West.

Next year, Cook expects Nurseryland alone to represent 20% to 25% of sales. Although he admits that it scares him to have one customer accounting for such a large percentage of sales, Cook said the increase in orders from Nurseryland will enable Springtime to expand more quickly. By the end of 1984, he expects 200 acres to be planted.

Other large customers include Target, Gemco and K-Mart.

Springtime was started with $5 million raised from the sale of three separate limited partnerships to 45 investors. Cook is the general partner. The land is leased to Springtime Growers Group. The landowners, who are principally interested in appreciation, get back part of the cost of owning the land through the lease to Springtime.

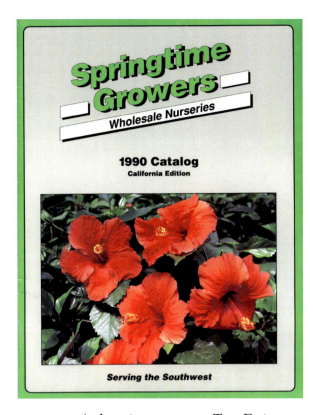

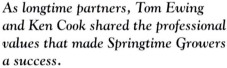

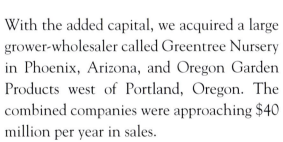

As longtime partners, Tom Ewing and Ken Cook shared the professional values that made Springtime Growers a success.

With the added capital, we acquired a large grower-wholesaler called Greentree Nursery in Phoenix, Arizona, and Oregon Garden Products west of Portland, Oregon. The combined companies were approaching $40 million per year in sales.

But while the company was thriving, the internal dynamics were becoming increasingly unhealthy. The purchase of Greentree Nursery and Oregon Garden Products had created a number of difficult managerial challenges, including some personal conflicts that were very disruptive. Working with Vista Ventures was proving to be extremely difficult due to their demands and lack of understanding of the business. I've always felt that work should be fun, and when it's not, something needs to change.

In the spring of 1990, with our last child, Caroline, leaving the nest, Mary Lou and I decided to sell our house in Del Mar and purchase a newly built home in Fallbrook, California. Our Del Mar house sold for $1.05 million. So far, the real estate market had been very good to our family.

Rewards in life are in exact proportion to our service.

The Cooks' Fallbrook home.

In the summer of 1990, we purchased a house at 960 Ranger Road in Fallbrook, on five acres just north of the Pala Mesa Resort. We paid $875,000, and I increased the value by adding a pool, tennis court and landscaping. Over a three-year period, I planted over 5,000 palm trees.

Within one year of moving to Fallbrook, I resigned my position as president of Springtime Growers. It had been an exciting 10 years building the company with Norm Osborne, Bob Forest and Tom Ewing. But the changes demanded by Vista Ventures were not acceptable to me, and that forced me to say goodbye to some wonderful, dedicated associates. There's no way to account for this on the balance sheet, but I have always maintained that your associates are the greatest asset of a business.

The women of the Cook family, taken around the time that Ken and Mary Lou moved to the Fallbrook home in 1990.

My Long History with Norm Osborne

have had many wonderful friends and business partners, none of whom I have valued and cherished more than Norm Osborne. I met Norm in January of 1974 when I interviewed him for a financial position with a company in which I had invested, Kolbeck Industries. That chance encounter led to a business and personal relationship that has lasted nearly four decades.

I got involved with Kolbeck in 1967 when its owner, John Luton, asked me to join his board of directors. Kolbeck was in the business of heavy-duty truck and motor-home frame and front-end alignment. At that point I was still quite inexperienced, and eager to learn how other companies were run. Gradually, I got more involved with the company, and was an active supporter of its move from downtown San Diego to the newly developed Miramar Road area in 1969.

In 1974, Kolbeck's accountant, Loren McElroy, retired. Looking for his replacement, we ran an advertisement in the *San Diego Union* that brought Norm Osborne to our door. Norm joined the company and soon thereafter became the vice-president and general manager. Kolbeck Industries was sold in 1980, and Norm and I started a long run of partnerships in various businesses, ranging from high-tech to low-tech to no-tech!

In 1976, we started Tool Shed Equipment Rental Company on Miramar Road. My good friend and former associate with Rent-It Service, Pete Clark, became the manager. Pete did such a great job that in 1979, we sold him the business.

Norm and I worked on the sale of The Growing Grounds to Nurseryland in the summer of 1980. In September of that year, we met Malcolm Crawford, an attorney from Denver, Colorado, who specialized in investment tax-deferred shelters. We developed a strategy, compiled an offering memorandum, and sold the $1.8 million offering in 10 days.

This was the beginning of Springtime Growers, Springtime Tree Ranch and Springtime Color, all operated under the Springtime Growers banner. The three offerings raised four million dollars, which was the capital required to make Springtime Growers a national leader in the wholesale nursery industry. Our good friend from Nurseryland and The Growing Grounds, Tom Ewing, became the vice-president and general manager. He and his wife, Debbie, became our good friends.

In late 1980, Norm agreed to assist in the growth and expansion of Cook's Corner. He developed our mail-order business and helped the company create a franchise selling Cook's Corner outlets.

In 1984, Norm, Pat Keig and I started Equishare, which built the Cook's Corner building, Private Ledger, Computer Accessories building, and Pointe Camino Research Center.

Norm was on the original board of directors for Computer Accessories (Proxima), and his contributions were highly respected. In March of 1989, without my involvement, Norm purchased Evergreen Nursery. When Signature Trees was formed in 1990-91, Norm Osborne became one of my partners.

In 1992 the CEO Group was formed, and we purchased The Pinery Christmas Trees. In 1997, I sold my interest in The Pinery back to Norm and his wife, Linda, so that their son, Mike, who was graduating from college, could have some equity. Today, The Pinery Christmas Trees and its autumn counterpart, the Pumpkin Station, are the most successful seasonal retail businesses in California. McKenzie Farms has had the honor of meeting their Christmas tree requirements for the past 20 years. Why? Because we share a value for quality and friendship.

Norm and Linda Osborne have been very close friends and business partners for almost 40 years. It's been a great ride — thanks for the memories!

Mary Lou and Ken with longtime friends and partners Linda and Norm Osborne.

Mary Lou's Cooking Awards

While I was busy with business, Mary Lou was accomplishing wonderful things on the home front. In addition to raising four great kids, she had become an accomplished cook, greatly influenced by her mother and paternal grandmother.

Over the years she has won many recipe contests, including the Pillsbury Bake-Off on three separate occasions. Each of her national awards, in competitions such as the National Beef Cook-Off, the National Chicken Contest, and the Paul Newman Recipe Contest, brought her media attention, prize money, gifts from the sponsors, and a nice trip. I was lucky enough to join Mary Lou on many of the contest trips, and I am very proud of her cooking accomplishments.

132

Mary Lou at the California Prune Festival contest with her award-winning Goldrush Cake.

*Ken and
Mary Lou at
the Pillsbury
Bake-Off
awards dinner
in 1994.*

Awards and Published Recipes

Pillsbury Bake-Off: 3-Time Winner
Pace Picante Sauce: 2-Time Winner
California Prune Contest: First Place — Cakes
Sargento Cheese: 2-Time Winner
Quaker Oats: 2-Time Winner
Fetzer Wine Salad Toss
Bay's English Muffins
Williams Foods
Oregon Beef Cook-Off: 3-Time Winner
National Beef Cook-Off: 2-Time Winner
National Chicken Contest
Paul Newman-Newman's Own Recipe Contest:
$10,000 for Charity
Good Housekeeping Magazine
Southern Living Magazine
Southern Living Cook-Off Cookbook: 3 Recipes
Better Homes and Gardens: Numerous Recipes
Gold Kist Farms Chicken Contest
Foster Farms Chicken Cook-Off

Cook-Gravo Construction

I met Jerry Gravo in the late summer of 1990 while Mary Lou and I resided in Fallbrook, California. He originally approached me with an investment proposal that he thought might be of interest to me. I knew the Gravo name in San Diego County was synonymous with quality home-building, so after turning him down on his proposal, I asked him if he would build a gazebo on my property.

Jerry agreed to build the gazebo and further agreed to travel to Welches, Oregon, to construct our new home there. He completed our home at 69315 East Rolling Green Court in the spring of 1991. Taken by the beauty of the Northwest, Jerry opted to stay on in Oregon, where for the past 20 years, he and I have been building homes in the Welches area.

Jerry honored me as his friend and mentor in his book *The Richest Gift*, an inspirational story about the road to prosperity. Jerry and his two daughters, Kaitlyn and Kelsey, are beloved friends of the Cook family. Jerry remains my builder of choice, my second son and very good friend.

134

The Cooks' Oregon home, built by Jerry Gravo.

The Christmas Tree Business — McKenzie Farms

In a phone call late in the summer of 1991, my good friend Gary Bishop encouraged me to get involved in the Christmas tree business in Oregon. A large Christmas tree grower, the J. Hofert Company, had made the decision to sell its holdings and close down its sales and growing business, which created an opportunity for another supplier.

Ken's experience in nurseries led him to take a major stake in the Christmas tree business.

After researching the industry, developing a business plan, contacting people with experience, and obtaining a line of credit, I decided to supply a limited number of Christmas trees to Home Depot, Target, and Wal-Mart under the name Signature Trees. Since we did not have any inventory, it was necessary for me to find growers who were willing to sell me trees. To help with that process, I retained the professional services of Mike Stone, a knowledgeable grower with many years of experience.

We conducted business the first year out of a motel room at the Burns Bros. truck stop in Wilsonville, Oregon. Mary Lou managed the dispatch and shipping office, I worked in the fields, and Mike Stone oversaw the harvest of the trees we purchased "on the stump." Dave and Gaylene Mann, who had experience in the shipping of Christmas trees, helped us when their work schedules permitted.

It was a modest beginning, filled with heartache and frustration. We shipped 130,000 trees our first year and lost over $1 million – for all the right reasons. We didn't know what we were doing, and even though I had purchased and sold Christmas trees at

Jeff Winslow and the QVC Channel

Gary Bishop, who introduced me to the Christmas tree business, was also the spark behind my brief experience in television sales. In 1994, he introduced me to Jeff Winslow, a very smart, aggressive and creative entrepreneur. Jeff taught me about marketing products through infomercials on the QVC television channel. Together, we developed two very interesting products, the Speed Toner and the One Putt.

The Speed Toner was a leg, thigh, and back strengthening device. Jeff and I sat in the green room of the QVC television channel in 1995 and watched as thousands of Speed Toners were sold in a one-hour segment.

One Putt was an attachment you could place on your putter with a mirror that helped in proper putt alignment. We did a number of infomercials and sold thousands of units.

Today Jeff has his own jet aircraft sales business in Carlsbad, California. He and his wife, Sherry, are good friends whom we enjoy seeing when schedules permit.

Mel Questad, whose knowledge and confidence kept Ken in the Christmas tree business during the difficult early years.

days a week for 52 weeks a year. After some consideration, I realized I was committed to succeeding in this business, and decided to give it one more year.

The second year, with the same players and the addition of Mel Questad, a good-hearted, seasoned veteran, we shipped 225,000 trees and broke even. In the third year, we shipped 250,000 trees and made a little money. By the fourth year, Dave and Gaylene Mann had joined us on a full-time basis and Mary Lou happily retired to resume her role as a loving and supportive wife. We made enough money to start buying and leasing land in order to plant our own tree fields.

After four years, I understood the dynamics of the business. We had a competent team of associates, a solid network of growers, an upgraded software package and a strong sales and marketing program. The Stockner brothers, Craig and Kevin, who managed a specialized Christmas tree service company, helped us with the maintenance, harvest and shipping. Our base of operations during harvest was the TA Truck Stop in Aurora, Oregon.

Nurseryland and The Growing Grounds, I had never shipped Christmas trees to major big-box accounts.

When the shipping season ended, I came very close to shutting down Signature Trees and continuing my life of retirement. To be successful in life you must understand the difference between interest and commitment. When you're interested in doing something, you do it when it's convenient. When you're committed, you accept no excuses — just results — and you do it seven

We also had a field office in a 100-year-old barn in Oregon City, Oregon, which we called Signature 1. In 1994, our fourth year, we shipped over 300,000 trees to distributors throughout the United States. We were now established, respected and had the finest quality trees in the industry. The tree selection process was my responsibility,

 Successful people are always looking for ways to help others. Unsuccessful people are always asking, "What's in it for me?"

Attitude is Everything

If you want to stay healthy and live a longer, more successful, happier life, you must maintain a positive mental attitude. The longer I live, the more I realize the impact and importance of attitude. To me, attitude is more important than knowledge or facts. It can be the difference between success and failure.

It is more important than the past, than education, than circumstances, than failures, than successes, than what people think, say or do. It is more important than skill or appearance. I also believe that a negative mental attitude can be responsible for the failure of a company, a family, a church, or a relationship.

The remarkable thing is that we have a choice every day regarding the attitude we embrace. Our thoughts control our destiny! We cannot change the past. We cannot change the inevitable. Present thoughts and actions determine our future. A positive mental attitude is contagious and impacts everyone we come in contact with. The more we give, the more we will receive.

I am convinced that life is not based on what happens to me, but rather how I react to life. We are what we do, and we alone are in charge of our attitudes. Every act is a self-portrait. With a positive mental attitude, that portrait will reflect us as we most wish to be: strong, happy, and productive.

which I only shared with trusted family members and associates. It was our goal to grow, broker, harvest and ship a "Signature Christmas tree," Oregon's finest!

In 1994, our daughter Caroline moved from California to Oregon. A few months after she began her job search, I suggested she work with me in our Christmas tree business. She began with a modest assignment, helping me select and tag the trees, but stuck with it and worked her way up in the organization. Today Carey is our vice president and general manager, a seasoned veteran who is highly respected by her associates and fellow growers.

Since we had a beautiful home in Oregon, Mary Lou and I decided to sell the "Cook Compound," our large Fallbrook house. We loved that home, but the maintenance required three to four hours a day of my time, which was just too much. We found a smaller, two-bedroom townhouse on the golf course in the master-planned community of Aviara in Carlsbad, California. In May of 1997, 7077 Tatler Road became our California home.

In 1998, Jerry Halamuda and Mike Vukelich, the managing principals of Color Spot Nurseries, approached me regarding the possible acquisition of Signature Trees. Jerry Halamuda had a minor interest in Signature Trees since the beginning, and he later became a major owner of the company now known as McKenzie Farms. After an extended period of negotiations, Color Spot Nurseries acquired Signature Trees. The business was renamed Color Spot Christmas Trees, I was made president of the company, and Carey continued in a management role. Having Jerry Halamuda as a business partner was an added blessing. He is a remarkable person, businessman, mentor, and good friend – a valued member of my Up-the-Ladder Team.

Our new business plan gave me the charter to consolidate the Christmas tree industry.

This would counteract a serious problem in our field: with so many small, independent growers, the industry becomes weak and easily manipulated by major retailers. We began by acquiring Happy Holiday Christmas Trees, owned by Conrad "Cubby" Steinhart, in 1999. Soon after that we acquired Fraser Fir Tree Company from Scott Porter. They became part of the consolidated Color Spot Christmas Trees. The three companies shipped over 1.2 million trees with sales of $25 million in 2000, making Color Spot Christmas Trees the largest Christmas tree company in the United States.

Color Spot Christmas Trees was well managed, well positioned, and very profitable. We were nearing the completion of an acquisition of one of the largest Christmas tree companies in Oregon when I was advised that the owners of Color Spot,

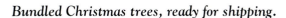

Bundled Christmas trees, ready for shipping.

Think Like a Winner

A Winner's Creed

What you do in life is determined by who you are.

Who you are is determined by what you think.

What you think is determined by what you learn.

What you learn is determined by what you experience.

What you experience is determined by what you do.

Success will come to those who are players in the arena of life.

Success will come to those who are willing to pay the price.

Success will come to those who never, never give up.

If you know what you can, you will.

Write down what you want in life.

Your sub-conscious will drive you toward your goal.

You must dare to do what you want.

If you can think it and see it, you can do it.

It's all in your state of mind.

We are what we think and do.

As I think I am, present thoughts determine my future.

A winner says "I can," and then makes it happen.

McKemzie Farms Signature Christmas trees.

Kohlberg & Company, did not want to invest additional funds into a business with an inventory that turned once every seven years and was capital intensive. With that news, I decided to resign my position and pursue other interests. Cubby Steinhart was named president and our daughter Carey was retained as manager of the Oregon operation. I was asked to stay on as a consultant for two years, which I agreed to do.

Carey was introduced to John Anderson in North Carolina in 1999 during a Color Spot Christmas Trees meeting. John's family had been Fraser Fir growers for many years and his father, who was a state extension agent in Jefferson County, was highly respected among the growers of North Carolina.

John moved to Oregon in 2000 and assumed the role of our production and field manager, responsible for new plantings, quality control, and management of the major mixing, shuttling and loading yard at our home office in Oregon City. John and Carey were married in May of 2001 and were blessed with a son, Jakob Anderson, in 2005.

During the next two years under Color Spot and Kohlberg leadership, the company became misdirected, which resulted in a loss of market share. Planting rotations were missed and the general morale of the

  Present thoughts determine my future.

The Team McKenzie Mind-Set

Don't tell me it can't be done, I don't have enough time, I am working too hard.

Just tell me I will do it, because I want to and I can.

The McKenzie Farms team. L to R: Dave Mann, Kristina Roberts, John Anderson, Carey Anderson, McKenzie Cook, Debbie Tedrow, and Tom Cook. These are all very special people.

company was not good. What used to be a hands-on, eyes-on business was being managed by young MBAs who had never run a business, never made payroll, and didn't know their ass from a hot rock.

In 2002, Kohlberg decided to sell Color Spot Christmas Trees, and asked me if I was interested in buying the business back. Together, Jerry Halamuda and I were able to repurchase our company for 20 cents on the dollar. I had originally sold the business for $6 million and now I was buying it back for $1.2 million. The asset value had increased by over $3 million. The only negative aspect

was that sales, which had been over $10 million with 500,000 trees sold per year, had dropped to under $8 million with 400,000 trees sold per year. It would be a challenge to regain market share.

Once the purchase was complete, we changed the name of the company to McKenzie Farms. Cubby Steinhart was interested in purchasing the eastern division, and I negotiated that transaction so that he was back in control of his original company, Happy Holiday. Cubby and his team have been able to build their company into a leadership position in the Midwest and Eastern United States. Today Happy Holiday and McKenzie Farms each sell more than 650,000 trees, and they have a strong strategic business relationship.

In October of 2003, we sold our house in Carlsbad and moved to La Quinta, California, near Palm Desert and Palm Springs. La Quinta is called "The Gem of the Desert," and it's easy to see why. We purchased a house at 49305 Rio Arenoso with the Rancho La Quinta Country Club. Six years later, we sold that home and purchased a larger one at 49880 Mission Drive West, which is on the golf course in Rancho La Quinta Country Club. We love spending the winters (December through May) in the California desert. There are good restaurants, outstanding golf courses, great

shopping and good friends, all within five minutes of our front door. When we think of scaling back to a single home, it will be to our desert retreat in La Quinta.

Soon after buying the Christmas tree business back from Color Spot, I got the opportunity to turn it into a family business. In the summer of 2002, my son Tom and his family moved from Ventura, California, to join us in Oregon. Tom, who had been in the brokerage business prior to the move, found that much like his sister Carey, he would have to start slow and work hard to learn the tree business. Today he is our sales and shipping manager, responsible for selling and shipping 650,000 trees per year. Carey, John and Tom make a great management team for our company, with other

Ken maintains a close connection with every aspect of the Christmas tree business, from the field to the customer.

valued and respected associates including Dave Mann, Kristina Roberts, Kris Kelly, Jose Villafania, Debbie Tedrow and Kerry Joe Stockner.

One of most exciting recent developments at McKenzie Farms is our association with Costco Wholesale Corporation. That relationship came about after a visit from a longtime good friend, college football teammate and business associate, Tom Kelly, and his wife Pam. About five years ago on a trip to California, they stopped by for a visit to our home in La Quinta. I mentioned Costco to Tom in reference to our Christmas tree business, and he told me that Jim Senegal, the president of Costco, was his high school buddy and still a very close friend.

After very serious consideration, Tom agreed to introduce me to Jim Senegal, and I presented Costco with a program called "Ten Days and Out." In order to minimize Costco's labor costs, we would sell our trees out of the back of a trailer on the lot, and we would only do it during the 10 busiest shopping days before Christmas. Instead of multiple species and prices, there would be just one SKU for all the trees we sold. Jim appreciated the simplicity of this concept, respected my knowledge, and approved the plan.

Based on my brief business relationship with Jim Senegal, I can fully understand why Costco is so highly respected in the big-box circle of companies. Ask any business leader in America to list the top 10 most admired and respected CEOs of public companies, and that list will undoubted include Jim Senegal's name. More importantly, he is held in high esteem by his suppliers, associates, and the Costco membership. In 2012 Jim stepped down as the president of Costco and turned the responsibility over to another talented leader, Craig Jelinek.

The Costco connection reunited Tom and me in business, and today he is the Costco account manager for McKenzie Farms. Life's relationships should always be valued, nurtured, and respected.

McKenzie Farms and Signature Trees celebrated their 20th anniversary in 2010. Over the past nine years, our in-field inventory has grown from less than 1 million trees to over 4 million. Our broker-network inventory has grown from 1 million trees to over 3 million. We now have an available inventory of over 7 million trees with an annual yield of 800,000 trees per year. The company owns over 1,000 acres and leases 2,500 acres; our network-growers own over 2,000 acres. With this inventory and current sales, we are the second-largest grower and shipper of Christmas trees in the United States.

The number-one tree grower in the country, Holiday Tree Farms, is owned and operated by my very good friends and competitors Hal Schudel and his sons, Dave, Steve and John, along with sales manager Greg Rondeau. Hal, a legend in the Christmas tree industry, recently completed his own very impressive autobiography, *From the Great Plains to the Great Northwest*, inspiring me to write mine. Thank you Hal!

Key Growers and Respected Friends

Throughout the 22-year history of Signature Trees, Color Spot Christmas Trees and McKenzie Farms, our success has been greatly influenced by the Christmas tree growers who were willing to share their knowledge with us. Valued business and personal relations played a major role in the birth, transition and maturity of McKenzie Farms. We shall be ever grateful to these men and women for their friendship and generous contributions.

Greg Rondeau, sales manager for Holiday Tree Farms, is a very good friend, respected competitor, and a leader in the Christmas tree industry.

Billy Barger is the owner of Barger Tree Farm. He and his wife, **Candace**, have been our close friends for over 20 years. His words and actions speak loud and clear. Over the years, Billy Barger has been honored by McKenzie Farms on numerous occasions for his many accomplishments on our behalf.

Don Batson has been a trusted grower and harvester for over 20 years. We at McKenzie Farms thank Don for his many years of dedicated service.

Mike Stone is a principal of the company known as BTN (the initials of his sons, Ben, Tyler, and Nathan). In the early days of Signature Trees, Mike taught me how to be a successful Christmas tree grower. I respect Mike's hard work, knowledge and contributions to our industry. Without Mike Stone and his partner **Bill Brawley**, I'm not sure there would have been a McKenzie Farms.

For over 75 years, since the early days of the timber and mill business, **Mike Park** and his family have been legends in the Estacada area. Mike was one of the first Christmas tree growers in Clackamas County. I respect Mike and his sons, Mike Jr. and Ron, and value their friendship.

Peter Dinsdale, owner of Blue Heron Farms, is a respected farmer, a valued good friend, an outstanding businessman, and one of McKenzie Farms' largest contract growers. Recently, Peter sold his Christmas tree inventory to McKenzie Farms. With each passing year, my personal and business relations with Peter have become closer and stronger.

Gordon Day and the late Steve Crosby and Brad Day of Cascade Tree Farm are pillars in the Estacada community. They hail from a family of high achievers.

  Life's greatest return is not what you receive, but what you become.

Kelvin and Dave Douglass are part of a respected family of Christmas tree growers which included their beautiful mother, the late Mrs. Barney Douglass.

Ed Seagraves is a former business partner and successful farmer who provided us with land to lease and trees to buy. His good judgment, hard work and sacrifices made him a very successful man.

Steve and Donna Barber of Hylo Tree Farm provided us with Christmas trees over a 20-year period. (Dr. Barber was also a highly respected physician.) The Hylo Farm in Salem was subsequently purchased by McKenzie Farms, which gave us a strong base of operations. We at McKenzie Farms value our friendship with the Barbers.

Ken Kraemer and his family have been growers of numerous crops in the Willamette Valley for over 60 years. Ken is a real friend to me and to McKenzie Farms.

The late **Jay Lamb and his wife, Pam Lamb**, have been doing business with us for over 20 years. Jay and Pam have grown some of the most beautiful Christmas trees in all of Oregon. Few men have walked the face of this Earth with higher values, stronger principles, and more positive energy than Jay Lamb. We have the greatest respect and admiration for the Lamb family.

Steve Rentfro, nicknamed "Reno," has been independently and successfully operating one of our largest Christmas tree mixing yards in the Salem/Silverton area for more than 20 years. He and his crew are very close friends of the McKenzie Farms family.

Charlie Grogan, his wife, Sally, and their son, Casey, with Silverbells Tree Farm, were among our first contract growers. Charlie's leadership in the state and national Christmas tree association established higher standards for our industry.

The late, great **Buzz Shannon** was a longtime friend and a respected tree grower. We both attended Oregon State in the mid-1950s. He was always a wealth of information, and we shared mutual respect and friendship.

Gary and Cragin Lowe with Raintree Farms have always been quality growers and quality people. We have appreciated their business and friendship for over 20 years.

Glen and Lori Lohr are valued friends who live in the George area of Estacada. We currently lease land from the Lohrs which is some of the best Noble Fir growing ground in all of Oregon. Like the trees on their property, our friendship and respect for the Lohrs continues to grow.

The late **Don and Betty Smith** were two very different and beautiful people. Their passing has left a real void on Springwater Road. Our friendship and respect for each other spans over two decades. We will always remember Don's inspirational poem recitals at our annual post-harvest Christmas party. He was and will always be an American original. Thanks to Betty and Don for some very special memories.

Elmore Mostul has been an inspiration to me. A longtime resident of Oregon City, Elmore is a man whose enthusiasm is contagious. He is a living example of Oregon's pioneering spirit.

Dennis and Kathy Morarity are true friends of the McKenzie Farms family. They are a tribute to teamwork, hard work, and the joy of a full and abundant life. We are proud to call them partners.

Craig, Kevin, and Kerry Joe Stockner have been our closest business associates and friends from the very beginning. We would not be where we are today without their devotion, hard work and contributions. We have been through a lot together, and yet we have remained respectful and very close. If you want to get the job done, and done right, you turn to the Stockners.

Ray and Melissa Weaver have farmed high-quality Christmas trees in the Estacada area for over 35 years. The Weavers believed in me and trusted me. Together we have made many multi-million dollar land and tree deals which have been mutually successful. Recently Melissa has been battling some health issues. Her strength, attitude and faith have been truly remarkable and inspirational to witness. I've always been proud to call Ray and Melissa my very good friends and partners.

Bob "Doc" Seivers and his family have been Christmas tree growers in the Monroe, Oregon, area for over 50 years. Monroe Tree Farms and Holiday Tree Farms were the early pioneers in the art of growing Christmas trees. McKenzie Farms has been working closely with Doc and his family to transition the business. We value our business dealings and our special friendship.

Jose "Angel" Guerrero is a new supplier, harvester and respected friend. His word is his bond, and he knows how to get the job done

Computer Accessories founders McKenzie Cook, Myron Eichen and Norm Osborne.

Computer Accessories – Proxima

In the latter part of 1980, our daughter Amy married Paul Eichen, whose father, Myron Eichen, was a highly respected "high-tech guru" in Southern California. Myron and I would meet from time to time and discuss business opportunities that were available for investment. Over coffee, we began to focus in on the opportunity for standardization in the interface-cable market. Most of the cables being produced were made in the back rooms of Radio Shacks, and therefore most of the quality-control issues in the early personal computer market were cable-related and not hardware issues.

In 1981, Myron introduced me to his friend Al Roshan, and the three of us would meet every Saturday morning to discuss, review, and develop strategy. We all agreed that there was an opportunity ahead of us.

That year we formed a company called Computer Accessories and capitalized the business for $100,000. In the beginning, Al Roshan was the only paid employee. We rented a small office warehouse, wrote the cable specifications, developed a packaging and marketing plan and started manufacturing cable in 1982. The marketplace welcomed our smart cables produced with high quality-control standards and up-market packaging. We quickly became the number-one cable company in the United States.

As the company grew, Myron's son Paul Eichen joined the business in the marketing and sales areas. A rash of competitors entered the field, and we had to scramble to stay ahead of the game. Al Roshan, with his brilliant start-up capabilities, soon became overwhelmed with the day-to-day management responsibilities, and passed the reins of Computer Accessories to Paul, who was made president and CEO. The company was renamed Proxima.

In 1985 Proxima began developing its first line of computer-data LCD projection equipment. Over the next 10 years, we became the industry pioneer and global leader in the visual digital communications market.

In 1989, the company retained the services of my friend Ken Olsen. Ken became CEO and president of Proxima, while Paul assumed the role of vice-president of sales and marketing.

By 1994, the company had grown from $10 million to $130 million in annual sales. Proxima was a public company and one of the fastest growth stocks on the NASDAQ. In 1995, I resigned from the Board of Directors of Proxima in order to make room for an investment banker whose knowledge was needed within the company.

In the late 1990s, Proxima was sold to Infocus of Wilsonville, Oregon, for $400 million. With only a small percentage of the proceeds of that transaction, the acquisition favorably impacted our personal net worth, and I learned a lesson about the importance of equity appreciation. We dreamed big and paid the price to make the dream come true. Yes, we built it ourselves, and though it wasn't easy, it was worth the pain and the journey. Many were rewarded for our success.

Myron Eichen, my friend, partner and mentor, left us on July 2, 2001. He was truly brilliant, a courageous and fantastic man. Thank you, Myron, for all the memories. You will not be forgotten.

Be cautious when people are greedy, and be greedy when people are cautious.

The D.K. Cook Heirs Oil and Gas Business

Among my latest business endeavors is one I came to accidentally, without much background in the field and without actively making the choice to get involved in it. That said, I am delighted to have been put in this position, and am thoroughly enjoying the learning curve. I have my Uncle DeLoyd to thank for it all.

My father's youngest brother, DeLoyd Kennard Cook, was born on May 5, 1918, in Elwood, Iowa. After graduating from college and serving our country as a naval officer, he became an independent petroleum geologist.

I remember my Uncle DeLoyd coming to our home in Oregon, asking our family to sign cards for a lottery on federally owned land. This process happened every year from 1948 through 1955. He told us that a few parcels of land were selected each year by the government, and the more cards he submitted, the better the chance that he would be selected to lease some potential oil and gas properties.

Over the course of about 50 years, Uncle DeLoyd would frequently show up at our home looking for a room, food and some companionship. He paid similar visits to his other brothers, his sister, and his nieces and nephews. He never offered to pay for anything, and we all thought he must be down and out.

Only in his later years did we learn that he had assumed a large number of oil and gas leases on properties in Texas, Wyoming and New Mexico. We also learned that he had 12 active pumping oil and gas wells.

DeLoyd Kennard Cook died October 18, 2004. He was never married and his last will divided his earthly possessions among his 18 nieces and nephews. After a rocky start dealing with the attorneys and disparate members of the families, we are now operating the estate under the D.K. Cook Heirs LLC. My cousin Fred Cook, my brother Richard Cook and I are the managing partners.

Ken's uncle DeLoyd Kennard Cook.

150

Allana Lorraine Cook
2 years

Marian Margaret Cook
3½ years

Donna Ruth Cook
3 months

Alfred Herbert Cook
12 years

Deloyd Kerton Cook
18 years

Allen IV Guiberson
3½ years

Candace Merry Cook
4½ years

Alfred L. Cook Jr.
7 years-11 mo.

Karen Esther Cook
11 years

Carol Deanne Cook
6 years

Donald James McNamara
25½ years

Kay McNamara
22½ years

Deloyd K. and Esther M. Cook
50TH Wedding Anniversary

Marian Esther Cook
2 years

Donald McKenzie Cook
7 years

Daniel McKenzie Cook
16 years

Marilyn Ruth Cook
23 years

Richard H. Cook
19 years

Don Allen Cook
14½ years

Maryland STUDIO

JANUARY, 1954

The 18 nieces and nephews who inherited the estate of DeLoyd K. Cook. This collage was assembled in 1954 as a gift for D.K. and Esther Cook, the grandparents of this large, happy family.

It turns out that our Uncle DeLoyd Cook was a very astute, knowledgeable and conservative businessman, who amassed an estate that is now worth between $6 and $8 million. As one of the heirs of the estate, I fondly remember the times we spent together, sharing a meal in our family dining room. This is a classic example of the old saying, "The more you give the more you shall receive." DeLoyd was the last living member of my father's family, and we all appreciate his gift and generosity.

McKenzie Cook's Financial and Business Rules

Never ever run out of money.

Associate with people who are smarter than you.

Always put the deal in writing.

Be persistent. Never ever give up.

Be willing to be different. Don't follow the pack.

Assess the risk before you commit. Don't suck your thumb.

Less is more. Watch the expenses and people's productivity.

Limit what you borrow. It must be paid back with after-tax earnings

Define success and always know where you are.

Be willing to reinvest your profits.

Know when to fold and walk away.

Commitment

Commitment is what transforms a promise into reality. It is the words that speak boldly of your intentions and the actions that speak louder than the words. It is making the time when there is none. It is moving forward with a positive mental attitude when the hours are long and life is a struggle. Your commitment means coming through time after time after time and year after year after year. It is never quitting! Commitment is the stuff character is made of: the power and will to make a change and make the impossible possible. It is the daily triumph of integrity over skepticism. It all starts with your COMMITMENT.

McKenzie Cook's Business Values

People are the greatest asset in business.

Hire smart rather than manage tough.

Hire people who are willing and able.

Attitude makes the difference.

Ask more of your people than they can do.

Don't accept incompetence – never, never.

Always be part of the answer, not the problem.

Communicate by words and example.

A business can consume as many people as you hire.

Never compromise on quality.

Concentrate on building market share.

The purpose of a business is to create a customer.

Price your product to make a profit.

Always share the good news and the bad news – no surprises.

A little success can create a lot of overhead.

Do your homework – a little knowledge is dangerous.

Provide a scorecard for success.

Never, never run out of cash – no matter what.

Leadership is the ability to create a business where people are self-committed, self-disciplined, self-directed and self-motivated toward accomplishing the business objective.

Ken and Mary Lou in Catalina, 2002.

Moving in a Positive Direction

Life never rolls out in a straight line. Most lifelines look more like a chart on the New York Stock Exchange – a few great highs, a few deep lows, with a lot of wavering in between. Some of the lows reflect mistakes we've made, and others stem from misfortunes completely beyond our control. What keeps us going, climbing out of those lows and striving for the highest highs, is attitude.

In this history, I've tried to be clear and honest about the turning points in my life, both positive and negative. I was born with a strong will and the ability to clearly see where I wanted to go, and that's been pivotal throughout my life. In childhood, fighting back from critical injuries in that car accident, or toughing it out through hard times, I was able to draw from an inner strength to envision myself overcoming those challenges. I firmly believe that we can all develop that innate ability – to control our thoughts and use them to move in a positive direction toward the accomplishment of our goals.

All through my life, I've set my sights high. That's often meant pushing myself to work harder, or do things that other people might not be willing to do. When I started high school, I was determined to be a top student athlete, despite the fact that I was not particularly tall. I got there by running and lifting weights every day, going beyond what the coaches required to find my own potential.

I became a leader in student government, on my teams, and later in my companies, because I was willing to make plans, identify strategies, and put in the time it took to accomplish my goals.

That kind of commitment can leverage amazing things. When I'm involved in a project, I'm consumed by that project, generating ideas and putting the pieces together to make it happen. My enthusiasm draws in others who bring their own skills and inspiration. A positive mental attitude impacts everyone it touches, and spreads out in all directions. The more you give, the more you receive.

I could list examples of that from throughout my career, but I'll focus on one of the earliest ones, Rent-It Service. When I first met Mr. Kuehler, I was desperate, willing to work a low-level job at a very low pay rate just to get a foot in the door. I gave it everything I had, and after two and a half years, I was offered the chance to buy the business. My father told me it would be insane: I was young, naïve, and didn't have any background in business economics. And in many ways, he was right – I was 25 years old, stepping into a million-dollar responsibility. But I was determined to give it a try, so I begged and borrowed enough money to do it. Those next three years gave me a clear understanding of my abilities, and a foundation for everything else I did in

Successful people are dreamers. They move in the direction of their dream by working hard and working smart until the vision of their dream becomes reality.

life. Without that move, I'd probably still be working for someone else.

In the same way that a positive attitude can boost success, it can also help you out from under your mistakes. The very worst event in my business career was the collapse of Cook's Corner. We were losing thousands of dollars a month, and I was under incredible pressure from creditors, suppliers, and my own associates, who were understandably concerned about their futures. I considered giving in to bankruptcy, but instead I opted to do an informal reorganization. We downsized our business, found a buyer, and I accepted my mistakes and financial loss. We visualized the best possible outcome and achieved it.

Like many failures, the Cook's Corner debacle became a stepping stone to the next success. A person must make mistakes in order to grow, and for that reason I'm always willing to give someone a second chance. I am what I am today because of the mistakes I've made along the way, and the people in my company and in my personal life are entitled to make mistakes as well.

Although a positive mental attitude is a great starting point, most of challenges I've tackled have also demanded a lot of hard work. If you want to achieve greatness, you've got to be willing to sacrifice with blood, sweat and tears. I was fortunate to have two wonderful role models for my work ethic: my parents, Ruth and Harold Cook. By example, they taught us to be responsible, to persevere, and to multiply ourselves

to become everything we are capable of being. Mary Lou and I have tried to instill that same ethic in our children, and I'm very proud of the way it's played out. It's not easy to work with your father, but two of my children and one son-in-law have chosen to do that. They're running the business now, as well as raising wonderful families of their own, living up to the high standards we set for them. Our other children are thriving in their own endeavors. I feel there's no greater gift you can give your children than the example of hard work and a responsible, productive life.

Our family business, McKenzie Farms, has given me more satisfaction than any other company in my long history. There's a great sense of accomplishment in the fact that I've built the business myself, with my own money. We don't have pressure from a lender or from a board of directors: my children and I make all the decisions. There were some rough times in the beginning, but all in all, I'd have to say these last 21 years have been the happiest of my life.

Over those years, I've become a bit more mellow. My children might dispute this, but I'm not as critical as I used to be, and I'm certainly a lot more patient. Also, I tend to take more time to make decisions. I used to decide everything on the spot, with very little reflection. Now I'll take a day or two, or even a week, to make a big decision. In general, I've become a lot more comfortable with where I am in life, and it's allowed me to relax and have more fun.

My Sister and Brothers

I have been blessed to have one loving sister and two wonderful brothers. Life is not perfect, nor are we all perfect. But over the years we have managed to stay close, sharing in the bad and good times with respect and love for each other. As Archbishop Desmond Tutu is quoted as saying, "You don't choose your family. They are God's gift to you, as you are to them."

My sister, Marilyn, and her husband, Jack, reside in Madras, Oregon. Jack and Marilyn were married on June 27, 1954, and have three children and eight grandchildren. Jack built the cable company in his area, sold it and retired in 1978.

My older brother, Richard, was married to Arlene Knappe on December 24, 1964. They were divorced in 1985. Richard and his partner, Heidi, live in Escondido, California, and have a townhouse in downtown Portland, Oregon. Richard retired as a stockbroker after being in the business for over 35 years.

My younger brother, Donn, was married to his first wife, Julia, on December 2, 1960, and they had five children. They were divorced and Donn married Catherine Griswold on April 16, 2002. Donn and Catherine live in Longmont, Colorado. Donn was a high school science teacher for 35 years in Tustin, California, before he retired.

The Cook siblings. L to R: Richard, Marilyn, Donn and McKenzie.

Ken and Mary Lou Cook and their children. Standing L to R: Ken, Mary Lou, Allison, Tom. Sitting: Carey and Amy.

Throughout this book, I've credited the people who've helped me along: my family and the business associates I've named over the years to my Up-the-Ladder Team. I'm also thankful for my religious faith and the strength it has given me. When I married Mary Lou, I converted from the Methodist Church where I was raised to Catholicism. As my work and family responsibilities grew, I became less active in the church, reserving Sundays for outings with our children rather than formal worship. But my faith as a Christian has remained unchanged throughout my life, and has had a profound impact on the way I think and act. I live by the Christian principles, and my words and deeds reflect that.

When I consider all the good things that have come my way in the last 75 years, the very best, and the one I'm most grateful for, is my wife, Mary Lou. She gets full credit for raising our beautiful family while I was struggling to succeed in business and keep the bills paid. Looking back on it, I wish I had more time to enjoy the children when they were young. But Mary Lou did such a good job as a mother, nurturing each of them to bring out their best qualities, that my sideline role worked out well for everyone.

I'm immensely grateful for our four children, our grandchildren and great-grandchild, and for the closeness we've found as a family. If you're lucky enough to have a close family and two or three good friends, you can consider yourself very successful. But as the next generation gets ready to take its place in the working world, I have some grave concerns about the state of our country. In my experience, to be in debt is to be in danger, and I worry about the immense economic deficit our children may inherit. I want them to have the same opportunities I had, to be able to prosper and thrive. Unless our country changes course very soon, I'm afraid they'll be facing a set of challenges that my generation never imagined. We must move this country forward based on the hard work and values of our founding fathers.

Still, I have great confidence that the Cook family successors will boldly forge their paths, bolstered by the wisdom and other gifts passed down through the generations. As we did, they will learn from the people they encounter, and from the highs and lows they experience. We can't entirely avoid setbacks, and we shouldn't wish to. It's all a great learning experience, and with a positive mental attitude, they will find their way through rich and exciting lives.

159

The Cook grandchildren.

Celebrating 25 Years Together

Good friends and family at the Cooks'
25th anniversary party. This page left:
Carolyn Parrack. Below: Jim and Lois
Hines. Facing page above: Ruth Cook
and Lina Scharnweber. Below:
Mr. and Mrs. Bud Quade.

A Shout Out to Some Other Special Friends

Walt West, a great high school football coach in Escondido.

Jim Ahler, committed and disciplined head basketball coach of Escondido High School.

Bud Quade, Escondido High School coach, teacher, principal, superintendent of schools, and a world-class educator and friend.

Chick Embrey, a spiritual leader, assistant football coach and head coach of Escondido High School and the winningest coach in the school's history.

The late **George Cordy**, a graduate of Escondido High School who became the sports editor of the *Escondido Times-Advocate*, a very dear friend to Mary Lou and me.

Bill Radney, teacher and principal of Escondido High School.

Tommy Prothro, our head football coach at Oregon State.

Palomar College coaches **Rusty Meyers**, basketball coach, and **John Bowman**, football coach.

The late, great **Andy Vinci**, who became head coach of the University of San Diego in the late 1960s and saved the football program.

Ernie Miller, longtime classmate, player and friend from San Diego.

University of San Diego teammates **Bob Keyes, Tom Chrones, Joe Manamara, Duane Rudzinski, Vern Valdez, C.J. Walker, Bill And Wayne Bourque, Ray Yoast, Joe Ditomaso, John Mulligan, Dick Gardner, Jack Garafona, Al Kish, Onnie Wright** and **Rick Novack**.

Coach **Paul Platts**, assistant head coach at the University of San Diego.

Mentor **Bob Mitchell** with Metro U.S. Construction in Detroit Lakes, Minnesota.

Mike Sill with Road Machinery of Minneapolis, Minnesota.

Ed Huxley, Hall of Fame architect and designer of Nurseryland, Growing Grounds, and our Del Mar home.

Bernie Levy and **Ron Pinsky**, two outstanding attorneys who were valued for their professional and personal advice.

Stan and Gini Brooks, neighbors and special friends in Del Mar, California.

Bernie and Joan Goott, good friends and neighbors in Del Mar, California.

David Diamond, business consultant, CPA, and friend who helped guide our course.

162

Steve Hawkins, dear friend and CPA for over 25 years.

Bobby Gunnels, a business associate with Nurseryland and a longtime friend.

Al Hass, a good friend, investor and our insurance specialist.

Peter Lawrence, a longtime friend and attorney.

Bronson Jacoway, a business associate, insurance provider and respected friend.

Al Monahan, founder of Private Ledger of San Diego, community leader and admired business associate.

John Lee, owner of the Kings Garden Restaurant in Solana Beach, California, who entertained our family for over 20 years with great food and friendship.

Bob Stander, legal counsel and respected friend, who helped guide our course for Intermark.

George Abernathy, an Intermark friend who was always there for me.

Joan Eichen, Myron Eichen's beloved wife, a special woman who is loved by Mary Lou and me.

Ron "the hammer" McRoberts, Mary Lou's brother, and his wife, **Michelle**, for the many good times we've shared as a family.

Norm and Marcia Ableson, our admired and loving neighbors in Carlsbad.

Carlos Barceló, accomplished fellow grower and a longtime friend.

Paul Behrers, my annual Maui, Hawaii, friend and tennis partner of over 35 years.

David Bowie, classic and successful jeweler, business associate and good friend.

163

Lowell and Marlene Forristall, deep Oregon roots, great people and respected friends.

Chris Hopkins, longtime friend, business associate and a respected industry leader.

Hoppy Hottmann, Bob Burton and **Marv Hollingsworth**, my dearest friends in Welches.

Steve Rentfro, business service provider and a longtime friend of McKenzie Farms.

Burt Whittenberg, business marketing consultant for McKenzie Farms and a dear friend.

  Individually we are weak; collectively we are strong.

Travel Adventures

Ken and Mary Lou have enjoyed many wonderful excursions in the United States and abroad. Right: London, fall of 2012, after an unforgettable Oceania cruise to Italy, Monaco, Greece, Montenegro and Croatia with Maggie Cox, Tom and Pam Kelly. Below: Ken frolics with the mermaids in Copenhagen.

Above: in front of the Tivoli fountain in Rome. Left: on an Alaska fishing trip with a number of other Christmas tree growers, Ken caught the week's biggest fish.

The Family Tree of McKenzie and Mary Lou Cook

Jakob ANDERSON
24 May 2004

Caroline Anne
COOK
26 Feb 1970

Dakota CASTRO
18 April 2005

Tyler DELBERT
29 July 1987

Allison Margaret
COOK
28 Oct 1965

Zack CASTRO
11 Oct 1998

Andrew DELBERT
11 June 1985

Makayla CASTRO
5 Aug 1997

Thomas
McKenzie
COOK
21 Feb 1963

Tanner COOK
1 Dec 2000

Kendall COOK
29 June 1993

MacKenna COOK
6 July 1995

Imogene EICHEN
3 Mar 2010

Amy Elizabeth
COOK
6 Nov 1961

Samantha DAVIS
18 Oct 2001

Noah EICHEN
29 Aug 1981

Rachel EICHEN
18 Aug 1987

McKenzie COOK
and
Mary Lou McRoberts COOK

UP THE LADDER TO SUCCESS

Richard and McKenzie's Iowa Tour

Two very important people in our family, who were destined to be joined in marriage, started their lives within 20 miles of each other. My father, Harold DeLoyd Cook, was born in Elwood, Iowa on May 19, 1901. Two years later, on May 31, 1903, my mother, Ruth Lavina Clump, was born in Emeline, Iowa. They both grew up on Iowa farms, working alongside their families to make a living in those rough years before rural electrification. By the time they met in college, both the Cooks and the Clumps had left their farms and moved into nearby towns.

My brother Richard and I share an interest in family history, and have talked for a long time about visiting the Clump and Cook family home sites. In September 2011, we arranged to meet in Iowa, accompanied by Heidi and Mary Lou, to see the places where our family has its roots.

Day 1: The Clump Family Home in Northern Iowa

Mary Lou and I began the trip in Minneapolis, where we rented a car and drove to Estherville, Iowa, near the Minnesota border. Estherville is the county seat, about six miles from the farm where Ruth Clump (May 31, 1903 – March 2, 1990) spent most of her childhood. In those days of horse and buggy travel, a roundtrip shopping expedition to Estherville could take three to four hours. Most farmers rose at 5:00 a.m. to make the most of each day.

My mother had wonderful memories of her years on the farm. She had just one sister, Irene, who was four years older, and they loved to pick wildflowers, go ice-skating, and camp out by the nearby lakes in the summer. It was a secluded life, but Ruth had a rich imagination. She could entertain herself for hours pretending she was the belle of a busy village, peopled by families she situated in the various outbuildings around the farm. Life was especially quiet after Irene left home, but around that time, a young boy named Dale Bosworth came to help out on the farm. Ruth became a real tomboy, daring herself to do everything he did. After

167

Irene and Ruth Clump, ages 17 and 14.

The Clump family headstones in Superior, Iowa. Above left: great-grandparents Frederick J. and Elmira M. Clump. Above right: Daniel Mussena Clump, Ken's maternal grandfather. Below: The barn at Ruth Clump's childhood home.

168

a couple of years, Dale got into trouble and ran away. Ruth was left to help her mother, Josephine, with the garden and chickens. Her father, Daniel Mussena Clump, became increasingly dependent on a hired man to help with the farm work.

When my mother was a high school sophomore, the Clump family left the farm and built a house on 10 acres in Superior, just a mile north of their homestead. Their move closely followed the dedication of Superior's new elementary and high school on March 26, 1915. Ruthie Clump gave a reading at that event, which was the biggest thing to happen in Superior since the Methodist Church was dedicated two years earlier. The board of education elected my grandfather, D.M. Clump, as its chairman.

During our visit to Superior, Mary Lou and I looked for the Clumps' home, which my mother had said was on the east side of town. Superior has about 50 houses, most of which were built before the 1900s, and others that were built in the 30s, 40s and 50s. We found one house from the early 1900s on the corner of 4th Avenue and First Street, but could not verify that the stately two-story was the one my grandfather had built.

We also had trouble locating the old farm. We knew it was situated at the junction of 320th Avenue (N-16) and 140th Street. But there was no farmhouse in that area – just cornfields as far as the eye could see. Looking out at those rolling hills gave us a sense of the bleakness and seclusion of my mother's childhood years. Without electricity,

Adam Apple

My mother's grandfather, Adam Apple, was born in Bavaria, Germany, in 1831, the eldest in a family of five children. He was educated in German schools and helped out on his father's farm. At the age of 17, Adam made the long and difficult journey from Rotterdam, Holland, to New York, where he served three years in an apprenticeship to a cabinetmaker.

In 1850, soon after gold was discovered in California, Adam joined the thousands of men who made their way to the west coast to try their luck at mining. He was quite successful, and in 1855, he moved eastward again, with money to buy property. Settling in south-central Wisconsin, he purchased a partially improved claim of 100 acres and lived in a log cabin. He married a German girl, Dorothy Eckel, and they moved to the Racine area, where they raised eight children and grew tobacco.

A photo from 1831 of Adam Apple, held by his mother, Barbara Becher.

The house believed to be the Clump family home in Superior, Iowa.

plumbing, or running water, the farmer's life in those days was not for the faint of heart.

Close to where the farmhouse should have been, we found the Little Swan Lakes Winery, built in the 1920s. When I knocked on the door, a gentleman came out and introduced himself as Scott Benjamin, the winemaker and owner. He told us an old house just up the road had been demolished 35 years ago. It's likely that was the original Clump farmhouse, built in the mid-1880s by Daniel and Josephine Clump.

It was an overcast day, with a northeast wind blowing at about 30 miles an hour. Despite the cold, we headed to the Superior Cemetery to continue our search for the family roots. After 20 minutes of looking at headstones, we found my grandfather, Daniel Mussena Clump (June 15, 1860 - November 19, 1924). Next to his headstone were those of my great-grandparents, Elmira Mitchell Clump (February 3, 1842 - January 28, 1927), and Fredrick John Clump (September 30, 1836 - October 23, 1929). Seeing more than 175 years of family history in that burial ground, we were moved to reflect on the hardships our ancestors had to contend with as they worked to give their children a better life

Before we left the area, we visited Oak Hill Cemetery in Estherville to pay our respects to Ella Apple Blakey, a relative on my mother's maternal side. I know very little about my mother, her family and her childhood in Superior. I wish I had asked her more questions about the people and times she experienced.

Day 2: The Cook Family Home in Central Iowa

From Estherville, Mary Lou and I drove about 250 miles to Maquoketa, Iowa, where we met Richard and Heidi at the Decker Hotel, built in 1875. After dinner and a good night's rest, we were ready for our journey to visit the home sites and burial places of the Cook side of the family. This would be a circuit of about 140 miles.

My father, Harold Cook, grew up on a farm in Elwood, Iowa, with his five brothers, Donald, Herbert, Edmund, Alfred, and DeLoyd, and two sisters, Ruth and Marian. His parents, Esther McKenzie Cook (June 18, 1879 - February 15, 1951) and DeLoyd Kinnard (D.K.) Cook (April 18, 1875 - November 19, 1958), were both college-educated. D.K. was a successful lawyer, prominent in Republican politics. But he and Esther raised their family on the Cook family's Elwood farm, which they inherited after the death of D.K.'s father, Edmund L. Cook. Harold grew up doing chores from early in the morning until late at night, and he never lost that hard-work ethic.

For our tour of the Cook family historical sites, Richard and I decided to rent a limousine, which would allow us to relax and enjoy the trip without the worries of driving. We began our journey at 7:45 a.m., heading to Cedar Rapids, where my grandparents lived after they sold the farm in about 1918. The street names had changed since then, but thanks to our driver, a policeman and a gentleman walking the neighborhood,

we found the house. The old address, 549 South 24th Street East, had become 549 Forest Drive Southeast, Cedar Rapids, Iowa.

As Richard and I walked up the stairs to the front door, we commented on what a beautiful home it was. It must have been one of the most impressive houses in the area in the early 1900s. The gentleman who came to the door was somewhat suspicious of us and of the limousine parked in front. But once we explained who we were, he warmed up to the occasion. He didn't invite us in, but did allow us to walk around the house. On my way around the back I noticed a rotten piece of siding and quickly pried out a small piece of wood as a memento. Richard

D. K. COOK.

D.K. Cook, taken from a campaign flyer announcing his run for the office of Representative of Clinton County on the Republican ticket.

The home of D.K. and Esther Cook in Cedar Rapids, Iowa.

and I reminisced about a family photo taken in front of the house around 1920-21. We wished we knew more about our grandparents' move from the farm to the city. There are so many family questions we should have asked our older relatives. Capturing our history for posterity is one of the greatest gifts we can leave our children.

Next we headed toward Elwood, Iowa, the birthplace of our father, Harold DeLoyd Cook (May 1, 1901- June 28, 1982). Elwood is a township of about 100 people. There wasn't a person in sight when we arrived on the main street, so we started knocking on doors to see if someone could direct us to the Cook farm. Richard and I had no success, but after a few minutes our driver yelled to us that he had found a man who was willing to guide us to the farm. It was a mile north

of town, on the south side of 110th Street, about three-quarters of a mile west of 185th Avenue.

The farmhouse, outbuildings and silo had been destroyed in the past 10 years. As we walked toward the building site, we noticed a pile of metal and wood debris, including a windmill with the type of generator that was used in the early 1900s to generate and retain electricity. One of the fins on the windmill was bent, and with a little twisting I was able to capture another memento. I also retrieved an old bed spring, perhaps from the bed where my father and his siblings had slept.

The eight Cook children attended school in Delmar, seven miles east of Elwood. As we toured the farm site, Richard and I talked about how they might have gotten there.

With no school bus or car, they probably traveled on horseback or in a horse-drawn buggy, or perhaps they walked all the way. In any event, the trip to school and to the city of Maquoketa for supplies would have been very difficult. Living on a farm in the early 1900s was one tough life, especially in the frigid winters of central Iowa.

Andrea Pote-Anselman, the daughter of my cousin Kay Pote, was kind enough to send us some pictures of the Cook farmhouse taken in the mid-1990s, before it was destroyed. From these pictures and from our visit, it's easy to imagine why my grandparents sold the farm and moved to town. As the children grew up and left, it must have

become increasingly difficult for D.K. and Esther to maintain the house and acreage. They deserved their retirement, and found it in that lovely home we had seen in Cedar Rapids.

We left the farm and returned our guide to his home in Elwood. I compensated him with a $20 bill, and as we left he called out, "You all come back now!"

From there we headed toward Elwood Cemetery, perched on a hill overlooking Elwood Creek and the township. We agreed it was a beautiful location and a well-maintained cemetery. The day was perfect, with blue skies and birds singing in the trees.

The Cook family farm was once situated on these beautiful rolling plains. The farmhouse and outbuildings are no longer standing.

D. K. COOK'S
GREAT PUBLIC SALE

Owing to poor health and the inability to secure satisfactory farm help, I have decided to reduce my farming operations and will offer on my premises situated 7 miles south-west of Maquoketa, three miles north-west of Elwood, 5 miles south-east of Nashville, 7 miles North-east of Lost Nation, on

Tuesday Feb. 20

At 10 o'clock a. m., free lunch at 11 o'clock, at Public Sale to the highest bidder, Positively without reserve or by bidding, the following described personal property

20 HORSES

One bay mare 7 years old, in foal, weight 1750; 2 bay geldings 4 years old, weight 1400, broke; 2 bay mares 3 years old, weight 1350, broke 2 brown geldings, 3 years old, weight 1200 each, broke; 1 iron gray gelding 4 years old, weight 1400, broke; 2 work horses 7 years, weight 3000 good workers. Bay mare ten years old in foal to Heir at Law the Great, gentle; yearling gelding, black weight 1100; 4 draft colts a red colt one gentle Shetland pony.

120 ALL NATIVE CATTLE 120

40 yearling steers fed corn 120 days, red and roan, dehorned; 20 yearling steers fed corn 60 days, red and Hereford, dehorned; 20 yearling steers, good feeders, some corn, red and roan; 20 yearling steckers, good quality, dehorned; 20 other cattle.

200 POLAND CHINA HOGS 200

One car load fat hogs, 80 head will average about 225 will be sold by weight, to be weighed at Elwood and delivered on either Thursday or Friday following the day of sale. 60 HEAD GOOD BROOD SOWS, all safe in pig to old boars. Two 2-year-old boars weight about 500 pounds each, 40 head of light Hogs, just the kind to run on grass or to follow cattle.

MACHINERY
1 wagon and box, iron wheel wagon, Deere divided shaft hay loader 2 riding corn plows, Deere ear corn slicer, a 15 bbl galvanized iron tank, new, tank heater, good wood rack, 16 ft harrow, stalk cutter, good as new corn planter, sugar hay rake, Babcock milk tester, 2 walking corn plows, pile of junk and old iron, some bed steads, rope, harness, side delivery rake, feed boxes, feed grinders, Champion mower, tools and equipment and other things.

TERMS
Sums of $10. and under, cash. All other amounts, one year's time at 7 per cent. on bankable notes, with approved security. Everything must be settled for on day of sale and before property is taken from the premises. EVERYTHING UNDER COVER. COME RAIN OR SHINE.

D. K. COOK, Prop.

COL. M. J. PINTER, Auctioneer   Maquoketa Record Print   W. S. HILL, Clerk

The original poster from the Cook family farm sale, 1918-19, Elwood, Iowa.

We located the monument for Edmund Loreston Cook (October 9, 1829 - February 10, 1915) and Ruby Adeline Chaffee (March 26, 1835 - August 1, 1901), my father's paternal grandparents. We also found the headstone for Robert Cook (September 2 1800 - April 9, 1867) and Ruth A. Kinnard Cook (July 29, 1803 - January 20, 1896), my father's great-grandparents. Richard and I captured the site on film and reflected on 211 years of family history. My father's mother, Esther Cook, is buried at Forest Lawn in Los Angeles, California, and his father, DeLoyd Cook, is buried in San Bernardino, California.

With the sun beginning to work its way to the west, we headed for our last two destinations: Delmar and Emeline. We found the school my father and his siblings had attended in Delmar, and with my father's 1919 high school annual in hand, we walked toward the building. Today it has changed from a high school to an elementary school. Some of the children, seeing our limousine, ran up and asked us what we were doing. As a joke, I told them we were making a movie, which sent them running and yelling back into the school. A minute later,

Ken and Richard with the headstone of their father's paternal grandparents.

the principal was at the door, ordering us off the grounds. What a difference one hundred years make! Today if you joke around with kids, you are looked on as a pervert. After explaining to the principal what we were doing there and sharing my dad's annual, she began to accept us, but never made us feel at home. After a few pictures and a final apology, we departed Delmar.

Our last visit was to Emeline, Iowa, the birthplace of our mother, Ruth Clump. To this day, we are not sure why she was born in Emeline, which is close to 300 miles east of her family's farm in Superior. Our best guess is that her mother, Josephine, was pregnant when she and her husband embarked on a trip to visit her parents in Racine, Wisconsin. That trip is about 450 miles one way and would have taken them more than two weeks. Perhaps Ruth came unexpectedly early, forcing her parents to stop in

Emeline for her birth. Today, Emeline has a stop sign and three buildings. Little has changed in over 100 years.

We returned to the Decker Hotel, pleased with our day's explorations, but all too aware of the gaps in our knowledge of the family history. The moral of the story is, ask the questions now, because after your elders die, it will be too late. Remember your pedigree, remember the old stories, and always show your admiration, respect and love for your family. Life is short but memories shared last forever.

I want to acknowledge and thank Justina Cook for her research and timely completion of the Cook / Clump family genealogy, covering the early 1700s to the present. Justina Cook is my brother Donn's daughter-in-law, married to Donn's son Matthew. The charts she produced are a real family treasure.

Edmund L. Cook

My father's grandfather, Edmund Loreston Cook, was born in 1829 in Ontario, Canada. When he was 12, his family moved to Clinton County, Iowa, where his parents purchased an 80-acre claim. At that time the area was primarily inhabited by Native Americans, and white neighbors were few and far between.

When he was 24, Edmund drove a covered wagon to California to join the gold rush. He was not very successful as a miner, and returned to Clinton County after two years, turning his attention to breeding and raising stock. He married twice, first to Emma Wilberger, who died just six years into their marriage after giving birth to a son, and then to Ruby Adaline Chaffee Sparks, who gave him three more children. Edmund was considered progressive and enterprising in his agricultural endeavors. By the end of his life he owned 360 acres of prime farmland and was an active, well-respected member of his community.

One of the last photos of Ruth Clump Cook before her death in 1990.

  May you live as long as you want and never want as long as you live.

Pedigree Chart of McKenzie Cook

Harold DeLoyd COOK
B: 19 May 1901
Elwood, IA
M: 16 Jun 1921
San Bernardino, CA
D: 28 Jun 1982
Escondido, CA

DeLoyd Kinnard COOK
B: 18 Apr 1875
Elwood, IA
M: 21 Dec. 1898
Elwood, IA
D: 19 Nov 1958
San Bernardino, CA

Edmond Loreston COOK
B: 9 Oct 1829, Welland,
Ontario, Canada
M: 16 Oct 1867, Elwood, IA
D: 10 Feb 1915, Elwood, IA

Ruby Adeline CHAFFEE
B: 26 Mar 1835, Dale, NY
D: 1 Aug 1901, Clinton, IA

Esther M. McKENZIE
B: 18 Jun 1879
Elwood, IA
D: 15 Feb 1951
Los Angeles, CA

Dr. H. Marcus McKENZIE
B: 15 Feb 1851, Bureau, IL
M: 21 Sept 1875, Whiteside, IL
D: 14 Jul 1936, Louisville, KY

Emma Marietta PIERCE
B: 11 Apr 1855, Truston, NY
D: 2 Jun 1924, Elwood, IA

Daniel McKenzie COOK
B: 10 Apr 1937
Portland, OR
M: 21 Jan 1961
San Diego, CA

Ruth Lavina CLUMP
B: 31 May 1903
Emeline, IA
D: 2 Mar 1990
Escondido, CA

Daniel Mussena CLUMP
B: 15 Jun 1860
Long Grove, IL
M: 28 Nov 1895
Racine, WI
D: 19 Nov 1924
Estherville, IA

Frederick John CLUMP
B: 30 Sept 1836, Buffalo, NY
M: 24 Dec 1857, Freeport. IL
D: 23 Oct. 1929, Superior, IA

Elmira MITCHELL
B: 3 Feb 1842, Long Grove, IL
D: 28 Jan, 1927, Superior, IA

Josephine APPLE
B: 6 Apr 1861
Racine, WI
D: 5 Dec 1940
California

Adam APPLE
B: 29 Nov 1831, Bavaria,
Germany
M: 5 Jul 1856, New Berlin, WI
D: 19 Apr 1905, Racine, WI

Dorthea ECKEL
B: 1 May 1837, Bavaria, Germany
D: 24 Feb 1913, Racine, WI

Prepared by Justina Cook
April 2011

Mary Lou's Family History

Mary Lou's parents, Thomas Hall McRoberts and Lina Alberta Robertson, were both born in Texas. Thomas (known as T.H. or Tommy) McRoberts was one of three children born to Katy Lou Hall and Asa Allen McRoberts. Lina (known as Dotty) Robertson was one of 13 children born to Almo Lee Robertson and Rosa Lee Shipley. Tommy and Dotty met in Fort Worth in the mid-1930s when Dotty began dating Tommy's brother, Allen. Somehow Tommy won Dotty over and they began to date. Soon after that, when the entire McRoberts family moved to California, Tommy and Dotty were parted. Tommy wrote many letters to Dotty (my wife still has those letters, which are written in pencil) and finally convinced her to come to Los Angeles, where they were married in 1936.

Just before Mary Lou was born, the young couple went to a movie at a local theatre. During the movie intermission, the theatre sponsored a lottery game called Keno, where Dotty amazingly won $500. This was quite a lot of money at the time, and they used their windfall as a down payment on a house in Los Angeles that included an upstairs apartment. They rented the house to a family of six, and Tommy and Dotty lived in the apartment. Mary Lou was born in Bell Gardens, California, on May 21, 1938.

When Mary Lou was almost three years old, Tommy, who worked at the United States Post Office, cut his leg on some metal machinery at work. Unknowingly, he had also scraped a mole on his leg, and from this injury he developed a malignant melanoma. Physicians of the time were not prepared to successfully treat patients with this type of cancer, and the diagnosis left little hope. Shortly after this shattering development came the attack on Pearl Harbor, and America was plunged into World War II. Tommy and Dotty suffered another blow when her two younger brothers, George and "D," who lived nearby and had been very helpful to the young, troubled family, both decided to serve their country and enlisted in the Marines.

Lina and Thomas McRoberts.

Mary Lou McRoberts, circa 1942.

Although there were times over the next few years when Tommy did see improvement and felt a ray of hope, the only real bright spot came when a second child, Ronald Thomas, joined the family on June 12, 1944. Ronnie, a handsome little blonde-haired baby, didn't receive as much attention as he would have in happier times. As he became an adult, it was noted by all who knew Tommy that Ron very much resembled his father.

Thomas Hall McRoberts, who bravely struggled through endless experimental medical treatments, tragically lost his battle with cancer when Mary Lou was eight years old, on September 3, 1945, at the age of 32. I regret that I never had the chance to meet Mary Lou's father because I know he was an exceptional person from all of the wonderful things that his family has told me about him.

In late 1947, Dotty, Mary Lou, and Ronnie moved to the seaside town of Encinitas, California, where the children's loving grandparents, Katy Lou and Asa McRoberts, were building a home overlooking the Pacific Ocean. The family spent two happy

Mary Lou with the family dog, Butch.

years there until Dotty, who was very independent and always known as a real "scrapper," found a tiny duplex for sale in nearby Escondido. Just before school started in 1949, with a very small down payment, Dotty purchased the property. She and the children moved into one unit and rented the other to cover the house payment, as she and Tommy had done in Los Angeles.

When the first renters moved out, they suggested that their friend Harry, a power lineman and electrician, would be a good tenant. The rest, as they say, is history. Harry Scharnweber, a strapping 6-foot-4 Iowa bachelor, and Lina McRoberts, barely 5 feet tall, began to date. Harry, who was also known as Slim, really liked being part of the family, and in about a year's time the two were married. Mary Lou and Ronnie were joined by a half-sister, Margaret Marie, on June 30, 1950.

Harry had quite a fascinating history. When World War II broke out, he was 37 years old and therefore exempt from the military draft, but made the decision to enlist in the Army. He wound up serving in Germany as General Patton's advance man, stringing communication lines ahead of the general. The winter weather was brutal and conditions were horrible. Years later, Harry became part of the electrical contractor team that built the San Onofre Nuclear Power Plant in California.

With his marriage to Lina, Harry became a wonderful husband, father and stepfather. He and Lina had more than 40 happy years together before she died at the age of 73. Harry lived on well into his late nineties. They both enjoyed many happy years with their seven grandchildren, Amy, Thomas, Allison, Geoff, Caroline, Joshua, and Sara. Harry and Lina would be delighted to know how their family tree has grown, with a current total of 12 great-grandchildren and one great-great-grandchild.

The journey of Mary Lou's family brought them from Texas to Escondido, where she and I would eventually meet and marry. It is fascinating to consider the many twists and turns that precede the point where two paths coincide, culminating in what is now our family history together.

Pedigree Chart of Mary Lou McRoberts Cook

Asa Allen McROBERTS
B: 9 May 1885
Kentucky
M: Abt 1912
D: 17 Dec 1966
Los Angeles, CA

Ashael M.W. McROBERTS
B: 13 Dec 1853, Triplett, KY
M: Abt 1875
D: 8 Jan 1944, Ft. Worth, TX

Lucy Ellen PEPPER
B: 20 Apr 1855, Johnson, KY
D: 17 Mar 1936, Ft. Worth, TX

Thomas Hall McROBERTS
B: 14 Sep 1914
Ft. Worth, TX
D: 3 Sep 1945
Los Angeles, CA

Katie Lou HALL
B: 1 Jan 1895
Texas
D: 6 Aug 1981
Los Angeles, CA

Rev. Thomas Hunt HALL
B: 29 Nov 1839, Merriwether, GA
M: 30 Dec 1893, Anderson, TX
D: 5 Sep 1914, HP, Brazoria, TX

Ella Virginia DAVIS
B: 24 Oct 1861, Memphis, TN
D: 4 Apr 1948, Fort Worth, TX

Mary Lou McROBERTS
B: 21 May 1938
Los Angeles, CA
M: 21 Jan 1961
San Diego, CA

Almo Lee ROBERTSON
B: 27 Sept 1875
Mississippi
M: 2 Dec 1894
Rains, TX
D: 2 Jul 1926
Emory, Rains, TX

A. Thomas J. ROBERTSON
B: 29 Dec 1853, Mississippi
M: 6 Nov 1873, Tippah, MS
D: 15 Jan 1909, Emory, Rains, TX

Nancy C.N. MEDFORD
B: Abt 1846, Mississippi
D: Abt 31 Oct 1881, Mississippi

Lina Alberta ROBERTSON
B: 22 Nov 1917
Texas
D: 3 Jul 1992
North Carolina

Rosa Lee SHIPLEY
B: 6 Aug 1875
Texas
D: 20 Sep 1968
Athens, TX

John H. SHIPLEY
B: 28 May 1853, Tennessee
M: Abt 1878
D: 3 Apr 1938, Snyder, Scurry, TX

Nancy H.N. MELTON
B: 21 May 1857, Rains, TX
D: 2 Mar 1928, Erath, TX

183

Prepared by Justina Cook
April 2011

Cook Family Christmases Through the Years

1964

1965

1966

1967

1968

1969

1970

1971

UP THE LADDER TO SUCCESS

1972

1973

1974

1975

1976

1977

1978

1979

1992

189

Our Children...

...and Grandchildren

A

B

C

D

UP THE LADDER TO SUCCESS

A: *Noah Eichen with Ken*

B: *Rachel and Noah Eichen*

C: *Noah Eichen*

D: *Samantha Davis*

E: *Tyler and Andy Delbert*

F: *Rachel and Noah Eichen and Samantha Davis*

G: *Amy Davis and Rachel Eichen*

H: *Imogene Eichen*

I: Andy Delbert with Ken
J: Zack and Makayla Castro
K: Tyler Delbert with Ken
L: Dakota Castro with Ken
M: Zack, Dakota and Makayla Castro
N: Makayla Castro
O: Zack Castro

194

M

N

O

196

P

Q

R   S

UP THE LADDER TO SUCCESS

P: Kendall and MacKenna Cook
Q: Tanner Cook
R: Jakob Anderson
S: Jakob Anderson
T: MacKenna, Kendall and Tanner Cook

A Cougar Without a Tail

by Noah Eichen

As a child growing up in Oregon, Ken used to run with the deer, the antelope and the cougars. Ken Cook moved with his family from Portland, Oregon, to California in the summer of 1950.

Cook always had dreams and aspirations of becoming a professional football player. Everything in his younger and later life was with the pursuit of athletic excellence.

Cook started his career in 1952 when he entered Escondido Union High School as a freshman with aspirations of becoming the best athlete in the history of the school.

His freshman coach, later to become superintendent of the district, Bud Quade, saw potential, took him under his wing, and fostered his growth as a student athlete.

During his sophomore year he became starting fullback on the varsity squad and played first string point guard on the basketball team.

Cook was named Most Valuable Player in football and basketball, and he made all CIF his sophomore, junior and senior years. But Cook was more than just an athlete. He became student body vice president his junior year and president as a senior.

"It was a difficult balance to maintain the demands placed upon me as a scholastic student leader and athlete."

Many coaches in the west began to follow his progress and scouted him his junior and senior years. During his senior year, Cook was offered numerous scholarships including bids from Washington State, Oregon State, University of California, University of Southern California, and Arizona State.

Because of his roots in Oregon, Cook decided to attend Oregon State at Corvallis, where the great legend Tommy Prothro, formerly of University of California at Los Angeles, was coaching. In an era where most coaches went to T-formation, Prothro was an advocate of the single-wing, with the quarterback blocking and the ball being snapped directly into the backfield. Cook once again excelled as a student athlete and was the starting guard on the football team and freshman class president.

Cook longed for California which prompted him to leave Oregon State, where his behavior as a wild and unruly freshman led to social probation. What was Oregon State's loss became University of San Diego's gain.

"In 1956, USD was touted as the Notre Dame of the west and I was very much a part of the plan."

Over Cook's tenure at the University of San Diego, they became a legend and NCAA powerhouse, with many of the players going on to professional football. Once again,

Ken Cook as an Escondido High School Cougar.

Cook excelled in the classroom and on the field. He was elected student body president at USD.

After graduation, Ken was hoping that the NFL would draft him and much to his dismay, he was taken as a free-agent by the San Francisco 49ers.

"The step from college to the pros is ten times greater than the step from high school to college in terms of size, speed, knowledge, and golden balls, not to be confused with brass balls."

The once great Escondido Cougar, Oregon State Beaver, and University of San Diego Pioneer realized that you can't always run with the deer and antelope, and that you have about as much chance in the pros as finding a cougar without a tail.

This article was written by Ken and Mary Lou's grandson, Noah Eichen, for publication in his school newspaper. It also ran in the Encinitas Coast Dispatch. Noah followed in his grandfather's footsteps as a star player on his high school football team, the Torrey Pines Falcons, and was offered scholarships to numerous colleges.

Don't Quit

When things go wrong, as they often will,
When the road you're travelling seems all up hill,

When the funds are low and the debts are high,
You want to smile, but you have to sigh,

When life is pressing you down a bit,
Rest if you must, but don't you quit.

Life is strange with its twists and turns,
As every one of us always learns,

And many a failure turns about,
When we would have won had we stuck it out.

Don't give up though the pace seems slow.
You will succeed with another blow.

Success is failure turned inside out.
Work hard, don't give up, and never have doubt.

And you never can tell how close you are.
It may be near when it seems so far.

So stick to the fight when you're hardest hit.
It's when things seem worst that you must not quit.

Author unknown
Chosen and adapted for my grandchildren

McKenzie Farms Team Members: Keep the Faith!

Doubt sees the obstacles.

Faith sees the way.

Doubt sees the blackest night.

Faith sees the light of day.

Doubt see the problems of life,

Faith sees the opportunities.

Doubt dreads to take a step,

Faith soars on high.

Doubt questions, "Who believes?"

Faith answers, "I."

Doubt says, "I can't."

Faith says, "Yes you can!"

By McKenzie Cook
November 1, 2012

An Old Irish Blessing

May the road

Rise up to meet you.

May the wind

Always be at your back.

May the sun shine on your face

And rains fall

Soft upon your fields.

And until we meet again,

May God hold you

In the palm of His hand.